God's Love
for <u>You!</u>

A Revelation of the Eternal
Heart of God

I0138383

Rudi Louw

For example, the apostle Paul said in his second letter to Timothy in Chapter Three, Verse Sixteen that,

"All Scripture is given by inspiration of God (literally God breathed) *and is profitable for doctrine, for reproof, for correction, for instruction **in righteousness**."*

Table of Contents

The Marvel of the Holy Bible

1. Uninterrupted Theme and Inspired Thought

It took *1,500 years* to compile the Holy Bible, involving *more than 40 different authors*. <u>Yet</u> the theme and inspired thought of Scripture, continues *uninterrupted* from author to author, from beginning till end.

2. Absence of Mythical Stories

Compare philosophies and theories about creation in the Middle East, Europe, Asia, Africa, and Latin America and you'll find mythical scenarios: gods feuding and cutting up other gods to form the heavens and the earth, etc.

In ancient Greek mythology, the Greeks see Atlas carrying the earth on his shoulders. In India, Hindus believe eight elephants carry the earth on their backs.

But in contrast, Job, the oldest book in the Holy Bible, declares that, *"God suspends the earth 'on nothing."(Job 26:7)*

This was said millennia before Isaac Newton discovered the invisible laws of gravity that delicately balance every planet and sun in its individual circuit.

Contrary to every other ancient attempt to give a creation account, *the Holy Bible pictures the creation of the earth in a very scientific manner.*

Example: In Genesis Chapter One, the continents are lifted from the seas then vegetation is formed and later animal life all reproducing *'according to its own kind'*, **thus recognizing the fixed genetic laws.** In addition, we have the bringing forth of man and woman, *all done by God in a dignified and proper manner, without mythological adornments.*

The balance or remainder of the Holy Bible follow suite.

The narratives are **true historical documents**, *faithfully reflecting society and culture* **as history and archaeology would discover them thousands of years later. Not only is the Holy Bible historically accurate, it is also reliable when it deals with scientifically proven subjects.**

It was never intended to be a textbook on history, science, mathematics, or medicine. *However, when its writers touch on these subjects,* **they often state facts that** *scientific advancement would not reveal, or even consider, until thousands of years later.*

While many have doubted the accuracy of the Holy Bible, time and continued research have consistently demonstrated that the Word of God is better informed than its critics.

3. Intactness

Of all the ancient works of substantial size, *the Holy Bible survives intact, against all odds and expectations.*

Compared with other ancient writings, the Holy Bible has more manuscripts as evidence to support it than any ten pieces of classical literature combined!

The plays of William Shakespeare, for instance, were written about four hundred years ago, after the invention of the printing press. Many of his original writings and words have been lost in numerous sections, *yet the Holy Bible's uncanny preservation, has weathered thousands of years of wars, contradictions, persecutions, fires and invasions.*

Through the centuries Jewish scribes have preserved the Holy Bible's Old Covenant text, ***such as no other manuscripts has ever*** *been preserved. **They kept tabs on every letter, syllable, word and paragraph.** They continued from generation to generation to appoint and train special groups of men within their culture, **whose sole duty it was to preserve and transmit these documents, <u>with perfect accuracy and fidelity</u>.***

Who ever bothered to count the letters, syllables, or words of Plato, Aristotle, or Seneca for that matter?

When it comes to the New Testament, the actual number of preserved manuscripts is so great that it becomes overwhelming. ***There are more than 5,680 Greek manuscripts, more than 10,000 Latin Vulgate manuscripts and at least 9,300 other versions. Further still, there exists an additional 25,000 manuscript copies of portions of the New Testament.* No other document of antiquity even begins to approach such numbers.**

The closest in comparison is Homer's <u>Iliad</u>, with only 643 manuscripts. The first complete work of Homer only dates back to the 13th century.

4. Unmatched Accuracy in Predictive Foretelling

The Holy Bible is unmatched in accuracy in predictive foretelling. No other ancient work

succeeds in this, or even begins to attempt this.

Other books, such as the Koran, the Book of Mormon, and parts of the Veda claim divine inspiration; *but none of these books contain predictive foretelling.*

This one undeniable fact we know for certain: *While microscopic scrutiny would show up the imperfections, blemishes and defects of any work of man, it magnifies the beauties and perfection of God. Just as every flower displays in accurate detail the reflection and perfection of beauty, so does the Word of Truth when it is scrutinized.*

Historian Philip Schaff wrote:

"Without money and weapons, Jesus the Christ conquered more millions, than Alexander, Caesar, Mohammad, and Napoleon. Without science and learning, He (Jesus the Christ) shed more light on things human and divine than all philosophers and scholars combined. Without the eloquence of schools, He (Jesus the Christ) spoke such words of life as was never spoken before or since and produced effects which lie beyond the reach of orator or poet. Without writing a single line, He (Jesus the Christ) set more pens in motion and furnished themes for more sermons, orations, discussions, learned volumes, works of art, and songs of praise

than the whole army of great men of ancient and modern times combined." (*The Person of Christ*, p33. 1913)

Today, there are literally billions of Bibles in more than 2,000 languages.

Isn't it about time you find out what it really has to say?

Hey listen, the Holy Bible is all about Jesus, the Messiah, the Christ…

…and everything about Jesus Christ is really about YOU!!

Study Tips:

Read 2 Corinthians 5:14, 16, 18, 19, and 21.

In the light of these Scriptures, it should be obvious that, if you want to study the Holy Bible, *you should study it in the light of mankind's redemption!*

Feed daily on **redemption realities** found in the book of Acts, in Romans Chapters One through Eight, and in Ephesians, Colossians, and Galatians. These truths are also prevalent in 1 Peter Chapter 1, 2 Peter Chapter 1, James Chapter 1, and in 1 & 2 Corinthians.

Acknowledgment

I want to acknowledge and thank one of my mentors in the faith, Francois du Toit, for blessing and impacting my life with genuine love. For in it, *I saw* the love God has *for me.*

I borrowed the portion on *"The Marvel of the Holy Bible"* from his website: http://www.MirrorWord.net, as students so often feel they have a right to do with things that come from teachers they respect. Just as Galatians 6:6 says, *"Let him who is taught the Word share in all good things with him who teaches."*

Francois, I want to give you the honor, respect, and appreciation you deserve for the indelible mark you left on so many of our lives, *and on my life in particular.* Had I not heard you preach so clearly on *God's eternal love dream, I am sure that I would not be enjoying such a place of bliss today in the bosom of God, my Father, in intimate fellowship and friendship with my Daddy, who loves me,* nor would I ever have written a book like this.

Because of what you shared, I am in love with Him still! Addicted forever!

Thank you, sir!

To all our many dear friends, and our precious family, whom we love, for all your love and support, and to Chase Aderhold and all those who helped me with this project:

THANK YOU!

Also, especially to my sweet wife, Carmen:

For loving me so much and therefore keeping me genuine, and for being my companion in life and partner in ministry,

I love and appreciate you my darling, so very much!

Foreword

Thank you for taking the time to read this book.

Let me start off by saying that *I am totally addicted to my Daddy's love for me.*

I am in love with Jesus Christ, *and that is enough for me!*

The love of God is so much more than a doctrine, a philosophy, or a theory. It is so much more and goes so much deeper than knowledge: *it way surpasses knowledge.*

We are talking heart language here.

I write *to impact people's hearts,* to make them see the mysteries that have been hidden in Father God's heart concerning Christ Jesus, and really *concerning THEM.* I do this so as to arrest their conscience with it, *that I may introduce them to their original design and their true selves,* **presenting them to themselves perfect in Christ Jesus,** *and setting them apart unto Him* **in love,** as a chaste virgin.

We are involved with the biggest romance of the ages!

Therefore, this book cannot be read as you would a novel: *casually.* It is not a cleverly devised little myth or fable. **It contains revelation into some things you may or may not have considered before.**

It is the TRUTH of God, ultimate TRUTH, and therefore has direct bearing upon YOUR life. **The Word and the Spirit are my witness** *to the reality of these things!*

Be like the people of Berea whom the Apostle Paul ministered to in Acts 17:11. Open yourself up to study the revelation contained in this book, **to discover for yourself the reality of these things**.

Be forewarned! Do not become guilty of the sins of the Pharisees, **or you too will miss out on the depth of fulfillment God Himself, who is LOVE, wants to give YOU**.

Jesus said of the Pharisees and Sadducees that they strain out every little gnat BUT swallow whole camels. What He meant by that is that *some people seem to have it all together when it comes to doctrine and they love to argue.*

It makes them feel important but it is nothing other than EMPTY religious and intellectual pride.

They know the Scriptures in and out and YET they are still so IGNORANT about **REAL TRUTH that is only found in LOVE.**

They are still so ignorant and indifferent **towards the things that REALLY MATTER.**

They are always arguing over the use of *every little jot and tittle* and over the meaning and interpretation of *every word of Scripture.*

The exact thing they accuse everyone else of doing though, the precise thing they judge everyone else for, *they are actually doing themselves.* That is, **they often completely misinterpret and twist what is being said,** *making a big deal of insignificant things, while obscuring or weakening God's real truth: the truth of His LOVE.*

They are always majoring on minors **<u>because they do not understand the heart of God</u>,** *and therefore they constantly miss the whole point of the message.*

Paul himself said it so beautifully:

"…the letter kills but **the Spirit BRINGS LIFE…"**

"…<u>knowledge puffs up</u>, but **LOVE EDIFIES…"**

I say again:

Allow yourself to get caught up in the revelation I am about to share.

Open yourself up to study the insight contained in this book, *not only with a desire to gain* knowledge, but also with anticipation **to hear from Father God yourself;**

...**to encounter Him through His Word;**

...**and to embrace truth in order to know and believe the LOVE God has for <u>you</u>,** so that you may get so caught up in it, **that you too may receive from Him LOVES' impartation of LIFE.**

This revelation into the eternal heart of God contains within it the voice and call of LOVE Himself to every human being on the face of this earth.

If you take heed to these things and yield yourself fully to it, **it is custom designed and guaranteed to forever alter and enrich your life!**

"O Lord,
You have searched me
and known me.

You understand (know, discern)
my thoughts.

You comprehend my path,
And are acquainted with all my
ways."

(Does this make you
uncomfortable?
Or do you understand that
God _still_ loves you?)

"You have hedged me behind
and before,
and laid Your hand upon me"

(Another verse says:
Underneath me are the
everlasting arms).

"Such knowledge is too wonderful
for me;
I have a hard time grasping it.

You have formed my inward
parts
(my spirit-being, the real me);

You have covered me in my
mother's womb
(That covering is not us;
it is just the bodies we live in)
I will praise You,
for I am fearfully and
wonderfully made;

Marvelous are Your works.
This my soul knows very well

How precious also
are Your thoughts to me, O God!

How great is the sum of them!

If I should count them,
they would outnumber the sand;

When I awake, I am still with
You.
(You have never left me!)"

Psalms 139: 1-3, 5, 6, 13, 14, 17,
18

"That which was from the beginning,
...which we have heard
(not just with our ears,
but with our spiritual ears),
...which we have also seen
(not just with our eyes,
but with our spiritual eyes)

...which we have looked upon
(...gazed at, beheld,
focused our attention upon),

...and which our hands have also
handled

(...which we have also
experienced,
not just in the physical realm,
but in our inner man),

...concerning the Word of life,

...we declare (make known) to
you,
...that you also may have this
fellowship with us;

...for truly our fellowship
is with the Father,
and with His Son,

Jesus Christ.

And these things we write to you that your joy may be full."

1 John 1:1-4

Prayer

I thank you, Father God, that You are not some unknown energy-ball floating in outer space somewhere.

You are not some strange and mysterious cosmic force of the universe!

I thank you that You created and still uphold the universe by the Word of Your power!

I thank you that You are not some mystical crystal or some stone we can hang around our neck either, some piece of wood or stone *carved by man's hands!*

I thank you that You are not some figment of our imagination. But *You are real, and You are indeed God.*

We didn't invent You in our minds. No, *You invented us and brought us forth out of Yourself.*

You are not some distant God in outer space somewhere, whom I can only know through some weird, mysterious vibes and feelings, or only in clinical terms, objectively according to Your external, eternal characteristics.

Thank you that You are **more than** a definition, **more than** a doctrine, *no matter how accurate it is!*

Thank you that You are not a God who's *afar off!*

*Thank you that You are a relational God **and that we are dear to You!***

You are not just some *unknown* person. **You are near to each and every one of us!**

Thank you that true Christianity is not a religion, it's not a bunch of moral do's and don'ts!

Thank you that our worship of You and our devotion to You *is not meant to be an obligation!*

Thank you that You are Daddy to those who discover You and their origin in You and relation to You.

We are indeed Your own image and likeness, Your offspring! Thank you that we can discover our very existence in You.

O Father, when I consider Your thoughts towards me, *how vast is the sum of them!*

When we sleep You *still* think of us.

You don't relent in Your love, or leave us alone, even for a moment.

We are not alone!

When we think about these realities;

...the reality of living and moving and having our being in You, who gives to all Men: life, breath, and all other things;

...when we think about these realities and we consider the fact that *You gave our spirits birth;*

...and that **You are in love with each and every one of us,** *and cannot get us off of Your mind;*

...we cannot help but exclaim in amazement, along with David: ***These things are so wonderful to us!***

Job says that Your thoughts *are ever towards us;* we cannot even swallow our spit in private!

Thank you that You are so near to each and every one of us;

You constantly take thought of us!

Like the sand of the sea *are Your thoughts in number.*

Your love is ever towards us!

Hallelujah!

Thank you that we are Your intense focus, **the object of Your desire**...

...Oh how overwhelming and wonderful!

I am so thankful for Your love!

I revel in it!

I appreciate You, Daddy.

I treasure Your very presence I experience even now...

I treasure Your love towards me and everyone else in this whole wide world;

*...***even the one reading this book right now!**

Thank you, Daddy, that we were created *to ENJOY Your presence;*

*...**to enjoy YOU!***

You are the *true fulfillment* of everything our heart desires!

Thank you *for the intensity of Your love and affection for us.*

It burns so strong, *how can we not respond to it?!*

How can we deny You in what You desire!

Chapter 1

God Doesn't Need to Change

Have you ever realized that God has emotions like us?

Paul said to the believers in Philippi in Philippians 1:8,

"I long for you all **with the affection of Jesus Christ**. (Not affection *like* His, but literally *the affection* **of** *Christ Jesus Himself.*)"

Paul is referring to the very real emotions of Jesus the risen Christ, *the One who is now totally united with the Father.*

To many of us, considering God in terms of *having intensely real human emotions* **is almost unthinkable.** But let's take it one step further.

In this scripture, Paul was referring to the *"affection"* God the Father and Jesus the Christ has **FOR US.**

Have you ever realized that God has *"affection" for* **YOU?**

That means: **HE HAS FEELINGS FOR YOU.**

HE ACTUALLY LOVES YOU *AFFECTIONATELY.*

GOD ACTUALLY LOVES <u>YOU</u>!!!

In writing this book, if there is one thing I believe God the Father wants us to understand, it is that, *in true Christianity, we are not trying to win God's favor or change His heart's attitude towards us.*

That is what religion is always trying to do, whether it is the man-made Christian religion, Judaism, Islam, Buddhism, Mormonism, Jehovah's Witness, or whatever religion it might be. *Through their own doing, their own efforts, their own system of works, they are always trying to make themselves a better person, more presentable before God.* They are always trying to win God's favor or change His negative attitude towards them.

God doesn't need to change, amen?! *God doesn't have an anger management problem!*

Just picture with me how, for years and years, there were all the nations of the world *with their own particular religion,* bringing their little sacrifices, *trying to win God's favor, trying to keep God from getting mad at them,* or trying to change His negative heart's attitude towards them. *Feeling themselves terribly unworthy and restricted in their ability to communicate with an invisible, out of reach, and easily angered, moody old God.*

The nation of Israel was no exception. Year after year they were bringing their little sacrificial lambs *according to the customs their forefathers handed down from generation to generation.*

Through their sacrifices under the Law of Moses *they were trying to win God's favor, trying to keep God from getting mad at them,* or trying to change His negative heart's attitude towards them;

…fearful to even approach Almighty God.

But then one day a prophet to Israel, called John the Baptist, when he saw Jesus of Nazareth approaching, he cried out,

"Behold! **The Lamb of God** *who takes away the sin of the world."* - John 1:29

Oh, how God, through John, must have blown their minds! Can you just imagine, after all those years of them bringing their little lambs to try and win God's favor, **now all of a sudden here is God** *bringing His little Lamb to try and win their favor.*

He came in person to love us and take away the sin of the world.

Let me tell you something: **It has never been Man trying to win God's favor.** *It has always been God trying to win Man's favor!*

When we realize this it defuses and removes all our struggles and striving, as well as our trying to at least have some kind of inferior approach to God. *When we realize* that it has always been God trying to win our favor, not the other way around, *it brings peace.*

Peace is what every heart is crying out for. The whole world is desperately trying to obtain inner peace, *but peace within oneself and peace with God* **is only found in the revelation of Jesus Christ and His work of redemption.**

2 Peter 1:2,

*"**Grace** (favor) **and peace** be multiplied to you in the knowledge of God our Father and the Lord Jesus Christ."*

Romans 5:1,

*"**Now we have peace with God** through our Lord Jesus Christ."*

Chapter 2

God Wants to Reveal Himself

The apostle Paul had such a passion for us *to truly understand* what is in the heart of God towards us that he constantly had a burning desire in his heart for us.

This was and is his passion and prayer: Ephesians 1:17-18,

17 *"…that the God of our Lord Jesus Christ, the Father of glory, may give to you the spirit of wisdom and revelation **in the knowledge of Him**...*

18 *…*the eyes of your understanding *being ENLIGHTENED (through the truth revealed in the gospel); **that you may** know **what is the hope of His calling;***

*…In other words: What are the riches of the glory, of **His inheritance in the saints**."*

What was he talking about? What is **the hope** of God's calling? In other words, *what is **He** hoping for?* **What does that mean for us?** *What can **we** hope for?* And, *what is **the calling** of God **all about?*** What is He calling *us into,* and, *what is in it for us,* and, *what does*

*He hope to gain? What is the content of His message to us? I.e. what is, **the truth revealed in the gospel**; what is, **the knowledge of Him?***

*What does He know, **and want us to know, <u>concerning ourselves,</u>** that we don't already know?*

*What is **the value** of that knowledge, **it's benefit to us?** ...**to Him?***

And, *what is **His inheritance** <u>in the saints</u>?*

Also, *what does he mean: **"IN US?"** ...**IN** the saints? Why call us **saints?** Why call us **holy ones?***

Ephesians 1:4-5,

4 *"**<u>He (God) chose us</u>** in Him **(Christ)** before the foundation of the world* (Colossians 1:16 & 17; Ephesians 3:9b) ***<u>that we should be</u> holy, and without blame <u>before Him, in love</u>**...*

5 *...**having predestined us, to adoption <u>as sons</u>, by Jesus Christ, to Himself,** according to the **good pleasure** of His will..."*

The word *"**chose**"* can be read as ASSOCIATED, thus,

*"God **associated us** (already) **in Christ** before the foundation* (or, *before the Fall* – in other words: **from the very beginning; even**

34

before God began creating, and *way before the Fall happened,* thus, *even before we created the world we live in) God associated us in Christ Jesus."*

That is why the prophets could talk about, *"the lamb that was slain from before the foundations of the earth."*

You see, **there is a powerful, *intimate connection, a close union if you will,* that existed** <u>between God and Man</u>*, in Christ, in the LOGOS. It was* <u>established</u> *before the creation of the world.*

You see, *Jesus is the authentic, original Adam, the blueprint Son,* **from whom and through whom and by whom** *we were made and brought into existence.* **We are made in His very own image and likeness.** That means that **our original, authentic blueprint,** *our* <u>true</u> *image and likeness,* <u>is preserved there in Him, in spite of the Fall</u>.

God refused to lose us in Adam, *because He already found us in Christ!*

You are irreplaceable!

The word *"predestined"* can also be read as PRE-DESIGNED or PRE-PLANNED. It means that, *you* **have already planned in full** *what you want to achieve,* **before you start.**

Just like someone will draw up *a blueprint,* before they start building a house. So when that house is built, after having dreamed about it for so long, *why would you not be excited over it and love it?* **Especially if it came out exactly as you had planned it to be; exactly according to the blueprint?**

God wants us to know that whatever age we are, whatever age you are, **you have a beginning <u>that cannot be measured in time</u>.**

You have the most awesome origin.

1 John 4:8 says, *"God is love."*

In the very beginning, before creation itself, before time as we experience it, before the existence of sin, before the existence of evil, there was in existence, already, a dynamic exchange of love, a relationship without boundaries, an intertwining, and an enjoyment of total abandonment. There was a being of such freedom, full of beauty and love and fullness of life, a being we now call: God.

It was in the very midst of this enjoyment, this life, this fiery love, at the core of this passion, at the core of this God, who is pure LOVE, *that the idea of YOU came into being!*

If love would dream, *what would love dream about?*

Only one thing: *COMPANIONSHIP!*

...Closeness, intimacy, connectedness!

If you could only imagine pure LOVE itself dreaming, *what would that kind of love dream up?* What would LOVE Himself dream up and come up with? I have news for you: **LOVE ALREADY DREAMT, *AND YOU ARE IT!***

The very imagination of God, who is love, *is our origin!*

Every invention begins with an original thought, and *we are HIS original thought!*

We are the expression of His imagination; of His thoughts.

We are the fruit of His creative inspiration, His initiative, **His intimate design and love-dream.**

YOU are Love's dream.

You are God's LOVE-dream; *the product of His* ***HEART!***

We are the expression of God's *greatest idea!* We are at the core of *the greatest idea that ever was!*

God, who is love, imagined YOU!

God is in love with YOU!

We all share **the same value,** *because we all share the same origin!*

Love and friendship only blossom *in an environment of* **appreciation.**

The word *"appreciate"* means **to discover, and then also to express, and communicate, <u>value</u>.**

We must discover our true worth; we must discover *God's value of us!*

Only then can we discover true value in one another!

God, our true father, our Daddy, *had already defined us* before time began! **He defined us as *His very own* image and likeness!**

We are all the same *and yet we are all unique!* We are all fashioned in the same mold; *the expression of the same thought.* **Yet** we are as different as two brothers in the same family. We are as different from one another as brothers and sisters, **we are every bit as individually unique as our fingerprints.**

God loves us all the same, and yet He loves each and every one of us, individually, *with unmatched, intense passion!* He loves us as individuals! No one else can love us like He does, not even our own Mamas!

This is one of the greatest mysteries of life, *one of the greatest mysteries of all,* how God could love all of us universally; the whole world, the whole human race, across all time, *and yet focus His love intensely, passionately, upon every single individual.* **He focuses His love upon each and every one of us, individually, as if we are the only person on the planet that matters to Him!**

It is true that God created the physical universe out of nothing. No pre-existent physical substance was used, *but He did use a substance.*

That substance is the *"LOGOS".*

That word *"LOGOS"* is translated *"WORD"* in John 1:1,

"In the beginning was the Word (the LOGOS) and the LOGOS was with God (or PROS – face to face; equal and intimate with God), **and the LOGOS was in very essence GOD, the essence of God***…"*

We get our English words *"logic"* and *"thought"* from this word *"LOGOS".* The word *"LOGOS",* however, denotes more than just a fleeting thought. *It indicates* **the totality of a thought.** Thus, the *"LOGOS"* includes the motive, the reasoning and development of that thought, *and finally the expression and communication of that thought.*

Wow! That's a mouth full! Ha... ha... ha...

The first word in the Bible, *"BERESHET"*, literally means: **IN THE HEAD.** And so, there, *right in the beginning,* in the book of Genesis, **we see how God's thoughts concerning creation, concerning Man, concerning us, went beyond a silent thought.** *It went beyond just a dream within Him.* **He expressed those thoughts when He created everything,** *and when He breathed as He spoke and brought humanity into existence.* **We are an expression of the original** *"LOGOS."*

Ephesians 1:4-5,

4 *"**He (God)** <u>**chose us**</u> **(associated us)** **in Him** (In the LOGOS that later took on flesh in Jesus. He chose us there in the LOGOS, in His thoughts, in Himself)* before the foundation of the world **that we should <u>be</u> holy and without blame before Him, <u>in love</u>,"*

"...that we should <u>be</u>."

"...that we should (exist)..."

"...that we should (exist) in holiness and (exist) without blame before Him..."

"...that we should (exist) <u>in love</u>..."

"...<u>that we should be in-love!</u>"

40

*"...that we should **be** holy and without blame before Him"*

*"...**in love**..."*

5 *"**having predestined us** to adoption **as sons** by Jesus Christ **to Himself,** according to the **good pleasure** of His will..."*

As I said before, that word *"**predestined**"* can also be read as PRE-DESIGNED or PRE-PLANNED.

5 *"**having PRE-PLANNED or PRE-DESIGNED US to** adoption **as sons** by Jesus Christ **to Himself;***

*...this was according to **the good pleasure** of His will..."*

The word *"**adoption**"* used here is not what it means in our Western society. It is not the introduction of a total stranger's children into your own family, and then accepting them as your own. No. ***It is a coming of age as sons,*** like the typical Jewish Bar Mitzvah.

(This whole concept of the Spirit of His Son sealing our sonship, *by echoing **Abba** "Father" **[Daddy]** in our hearts,* is talked about in more detail in Galatians 4:1-6.

*That echo in our hearts of our sonship, **that sealing of it in our hearts** by the Spirit of God* is the word *"HUIOTHESIA".*

41

I suggest you go read Galatians 4:1-6 *in the Mirror Bible.* It is so beautiful and clear there.

Ephesians 1:5 says,

5 *"having PRE-PLANNED or PRE-DESIGNED US for Himself, as sons, (to the adoption, or for the coming of age as sons), by Jesus Christ;*

...this was according to the good pleasure of His will..."

"All of creation is eagerly waiting in anticipation, (it is almost as with bated breath that creation itself is waiting), for the full manifestation of the sons of God" - Romans 8:19

In Acts 17:22-31, the apostle Paul talks about this fact that we were *pre-planned* and *pre-designed according to the good pleasure of our Father's will,* and he also talks about this coming of age as sons, *by the resurrection of Jesus Christ.*

But he first starts off talking about how we were *pre-planned* and *pre-designed according to the good pleasure of our Father's will,* and so he explains *this mysterious association* talked about there in Ephesians 1:4.

He discloses *this powerful connection* that exists between Man and God, in Christ Jesus, revealing *our existence in Him.*

42

He explains **how close every single one of us are to God's heart,** *even though most of us don't even know it.* But let's read it there;

Acts 17:22-31,

22 "Then Paul stood in the midst of the Areopagus and said, 'Men of Athens, I perceive that in all things you are sincerely religious..."

Note that **religion can be defined as:** *Man's best efforts to try and define and know God.*

The only problem with that is that God happens to live *in the unseen realm of reality,* **and thus cannot be seen with the naked eye.**

Therefore all religion is deeply flawed.

Our best attempts, no matter how sincere, *only lead to the* **wrong conclusions.** *Every definition* **falls short; it is inaccurate. Or even worse,** *it is* **totally wrong!**

Religion is *the vain attempts of fallen, confused humanity, who lost their way,* **to try and get back to** *a relationship* **with a God whom they cannot see.**

They know He exists, **but unless He reveals Himself, they cannot know Him,** *because they no longer have a relationship. In fact,* *they have not had a relationship with Him for a long long time, since creation itself, and the fall of Adam.*

Religion is a stranger's way of trying to define and know God. *Their best effort <u>is still a guess</u>.*

Acts 17:22-31,

22 *"'Men of Athens, I perceive that in all things you are very religious* (**very desirous to glorify God, and to know Him, and please Him**).

23 *For as I was passing through and considering the objects of worship, I even found an altar with this inscription:*

'TO THE UNKNOWN GOD.'"

They were searching after God, trying to define Him, trying to know Him, and they had come up with all sorts of definitions of what God is, and what He may be like.

But at the end of all their research and philosophizing, trying to define and know God, and glorify Him, they had to admit that perhaps they were no closer than when they started.

After all, **who can know the unknown?**

So, *just in case they were wrong in every one of their assumptions, and may have offended*

44

Him by their efforts, they erected an altar dedicated to, *'THE UNKNOWN GOD'.*

This is exactly where Paul starts his conversation with them. He puts them at ease, and he essentially says to them that,

'I want to commend you on your efforts because I can see that you are truly sincere.'

He was not mocking them or knocking their religious efforts, or talking down to them and sarcastically patronizing them. No, on the contrary, *all he could see was* **their desire after God.**

He was moved with love for them, because he knew that if they only knew what he knew, **how God had come and revealed Himself to us, and revealed our origin and design to us, in Jesus Christ**, *they would not have to search anymore,* for yet another inaccurate definition.

And they would finally be able to know themselves, their true selves, and to know God, and they would be able to interact with Him for who He actually is, *instead of having to guess, and be afraid of offending Him.*

So Paul says,

"Therefore, the One whom you worship without knowing, Him I proclaim to you:"

24 *"God, who made the world and everything in it, **since He is Lord of heaven and earth, does not dwell in temples made with hands."***

In other words: **He is everywhere and He is not interested in dwelling in buildings.**

25 *"Nor is He worshiped **with Men's hands**…"*

In other words: **He is not interested in religious works of service either**. **It does not give Him any pleasure. He is not interested in religious do's and don'ts and obligations** *"…as though He needed anything!"*

He honestly doesn't need anything from us.

All He wants to do is embrace us and add to us out of His fullness, and to share that love and fullness with us.

*"…since **He gives to all, life, breath, and all other things**."*

26 *"And He has made from one blood…"*

(From one man, Adam – or, **from one substance**… You see because the word *"blood"* is not in many of the earlier manuscripts, it should really read more accurately):

*"He has made **from One**…"*

(From one substance, from one source, the *"LOGOS,"* from Christ Jesus Himself) *"...every nation of men to dwell on all the face of the earth;"*

"...and has determined their pre-appointed times and the boundaries of their habitation,"

27 **"so that they should seek the Lord, in the hope <u>that they might</u> grope for Him and <u>find Him</u>, (or embrace Him)"**

"...though <u>He is not far from each one of us</u>;"

Isn't it marvelous to discover that God, *your real origin, the One who brought you into existence, your real Daddy, has a hope in His heart that we would grope for Him and find Him, or embrace Him,* **because He is not far from each and every one of us?**

Isn't it wonderful that **He is near us, right now?!** That **He is already closer to you** than *your next breath?!*

In fact, without His closeness and nearness *you would not even have a next breath,* because, *"...all things consist in Him and are being held together by the word of His power,"* **by His very power, by the very "LOGOS."**

He is closer to you right now than your very breath!

It is also astounding to me how religion always **wants to *exclude* people,** to *see them as* ***separated from God altogether,*** *and place them somehow* **outside of God's influence and reach.**

Yet here in Acts 17 **Paul was *fully* including these people, these HEATHEN, *in his conversation,* and revealing them to be *within God's embrace,* and *under God's influence already!***

*...**well at least to some degree**.*

Paul goes on to say,

28 *"**for in Him we live and move and have our being;***

*"...**just as also some of your own poets have said,**"*

*"...**For we are indeed His offspring.**"*

I am so glad Paul didn't limit himself to only quote from the Scriptures. He felt free enough to also quote from some other source *if it could give him a connection point and help people relate to his message,* even if he didn't always agree with everything else that source thought and said.

Paul understood that God is always communicating *in everything* and that God's message *is everywhere.* All he had to do was pay attention and look for it. *It wasn't that hard to find.*

*Once you recognize the voice of God, **you hear Him everywhere!***

Paul was quoting a Cilician Stoic Philosopher and Poet named Aratus, *whom these religious philosophers of Athens all highly esteemed.*

Aratus lived around 300 BC. Aratus was referring to yet another poem written by Epimenides from Kossos (Crete) who lived somewhere around 700 or 600 BC. In the two poems from both Epimenides and Aratus, on Radamanthus and Minos, supposedly, Minus, the son of Zeus was praising Zeus, the supreme God in Greek Mythology. Now that will totally mess with some religious theologians! Ha... ha... ha...

Paul recognized that the Spirit of Christ is the Spirit of prophecy, and that that Spirit, the prophetic Spirit of Christ, inspired men of old, just as He does today, and He found expression, *even in the poetry of the heathen!*

It is surprising to note that God was silent in Israel for a period of 400 years before Christ. There was no prophet in Israel for 400 years, or until the days of John the Baptist and Jesus.

*God was, in His silence, indicating **the inaccuracy** and **the deafness** and **blindness** of His servants under the Law, and of His* chosen people, Israel, and also **the dying away** of the old religious system. He was about to replace the Law given to Moses, as well as the religious system built around it, **with a far more accurate representation of TRUTH.**

He was about to come in person *to reveal TRUTH* **and** *to reveal Himself.*

So God was silent in Israel from about 400 BC, *and yet this Aratus, a Gentile, a heathen,* who lived around 300 BC, studying and old poem, *by reflection and pondering,* **discovered and tapped into the TRUTH.**

And so, **by inspiration of God,** he said,

'In Him we live and move and have our being, **for we are also His offspring***...'*

Now note how Paul, **using this truth** both *Epimenides and Aratus discovered,* **as a foundation** to launch out from, starts his message to them.

He says in Acts 17:29,

"Therefore, SINCE WE ARE the offspring of God, *we ought not to think that the Divine Nature is like gold or silver or stone, or something shaped by art* **and Man's devising***."*

We didn't invent God. God invented us and so *we have no right to* **our own inferior concepts and inaccurate interpretations of who He is, and who we are.**

It does not glorify Him. **It actually diminishes His glory.**

BUT He is not mad at you, *He knows you did it ignorantly.* **And so I have** <u>fabulous</u> *news* **for you!**

30 *"Truly, these times of ignorance God overlooked,* <u>*but now*</u> *He commands…*

(based on what He did for all Men, and based on He Himself revealing TRUTH more accurately, <u>*He insists on*</u>*)* <u>*all Men everywhere to repent."*</u>

He desires all Men, all people, to *"METANOIA"*, in the original language – **to have a change of mind.** To come to different conclusions; to a more accurate conclusion, and so, *to change their opinion about Him, and about themselves and about one another,* in order to change their attitudes and actions towards Him and towards themselves and towards others.

Because all their ignorant, religious attempts and thoughts and opinions **were wrong,** *no matter how sincere it was.* **It missed the mark, it was inaccurate!**

Why did God overlook Man's ignorance and didn't hold it against us?

Because the TRUTH about Him, in relation to us, and the TRUTH about us, as He knows us, *had not yet been revealed.*

But then He came in person; in Jesus Christ, and revealed Himself, and revealed us to us. He revealed the TRUTH about Himself and about us, and we no longer have a reason to continue in ignorance.

That is why He can pronounce with such bold confidence that all Men everywhere can and should now repent – or go through a METANOIA, a METAMORPH, a metamorphosis *of thinking and being,* a total change and transformation and renewal of mind, attitudes and actions.

Acts 17:31,

"…because He has appointed a day on which He judged the whole world in righteousness (He made a righteous judgment: He judged us all as righteous), by the Man (Jesus) whom He has ordained."

"He has given assurance of this to all (to every single one of us), by raising Him (Jesus) from the dead."

Romans 4:25 says that,

"He was delivered up (to death) **because of** *our offenses* (because we killed Him), *and was raised* (by God Himself) **because of** *our justification;* **because of** *our righteousness* (**because we were declared righteous - _our original righteousness was restored to us as a gift_**)*"*

Both Peter and Paul emphasized **this conclusion** elsewhere in Scripture! Read Acts 10:28; Acts 11:5-9, and 2 Corinthians 5:14 & 16.

That is why I took the liberty of changing the New King James Translation in this previous verse [Acts 17:31], because it clearly states in the Greek that Paul is talking about **the judgment _which already took place_ in Jesus Christ, and its verdict of righteousness restored,** *and not some future judgment to come.*

Now hold your horses just a minute!

Before you get all bent out of shape trying to defend *your doctrine* and wanting to defend your opinion on *the judgment to come,* listen carefully.

I didn't mention anything about there **not** being some kind of *a judgment to come,* now did I? I am not speaking against all future judgment, *I am just showing you what Paul* **was actually talking about** *here in Acts 17:31.*

He was talking about the fact that God is not the One judging us. He already declared us RIGHTEOUS. We judge and exclude and condemn ourselves!

Ha... ha... ha... Listen you don't have to try and defend truth. Truth is like a giant Grizzly Bear: *it can defend itself.*

The God of all truth is perfectly capable *of speaking for Himself.* He doesn't need your help, *so relax Max!*

There is a present and future judgment, if you want to call it such, *it's a judgment that people choose to live under, and* **they place it upon themselves! It's a hell of our own making** *and the Scriptures have much to say about it!*

However, God's judgment of us already took place in Christ Jesus! *He already concluded His judgment of us!*

If there is going to be any future judgment it is not going to come from God.

It is we who judge ourselves! We live under our own judgment; *under our own cloud of condemnation.* Any future judgment that takes place *comes from us:* **We judge ourselves unworthy of eternal life and exclude ourselves!**

But let's get off of that subject before someone tries to stone me. *I want you to focus now.* I do not want you to get all distracted by getting all offended now, and jumping to inaccurate conclusions about me. You have no idea what I believe in full, based on a few small statements I make in this book, so stop jumping to conclusions and *putting words in my mouth I didn't say!*

I am merely quoting Paul, here in Acts 17:31, and it is vital *for us all* <u>to see what he is saying</u>.

Read the first part of that Scripture again from Acts 17:22 up to verse 30 *so you don't miss out on **the point** Paul is making here.*

He was leading up to verse 31 <u>as a conclusion</u>!

Paul started off by saying,

*"...**the One whom you worship without knowing**, Him I now proclaim to you."*

Paul's whole message <u>is God's own conclusion of our value and worth</u> *because of our origin in Him, because He is our Daddy.*

Paul basically says that **God established our true identity and our value and worth to Him *and brought it to a final conclusion and exclamation mark in His Son, when God Himself took our sin and our judgment upon Himself and died there on that cross!***

He concluded His love for us and our belonging to Him, *in that Jesus not only died our death, but was raised from the dead, **as proof to us, of our eternal righteousness!***

*...**as proof that we have already been declared righteous, in the eternal ages past, and that we have been given that righteousness as a gift.***

He thus reaffirmed and restored our original righteousness to us!

Jesus gave us proof that Father God holds nothing against us!

"...that the times of ignorance, and all that resulted from it; all its fruit and consequences, have been truly, rightly, overlooked!"

...and therefore matters not at all!

<u>All that matters now</u> is that we know and embrace the TRUTH,

...that we know and embrace HIM; our *TRUE Father, <u>our DADDY</u>!*

It is astonishing to me how easily we develop the wrong picture of God, and sometimes a seriously warped one at that. **I dare say that most religious people do not know the God they worship.** *God remains a mystery to them.*

God doesn't want us to worship some false image of Him, which we came up with, through of a warped view of Him.

John 4:24 says,

*"God is Spirit, and those who worship Him must worship **in spirit and truth**."*

God wants Mankind to worship Him, to admire Him, *from an accurate understanding of The Truth!*

God wants Mankind to worship Him, to admire Him, for who He truly is!

Our spirits <u>engaged in His TRUTH</u> and <u>engaged in His Spirit</u>, that is the most accurate form of worship and devotion!

God is a person, *not some cruel ogre.* **He is the *living* God**, *not some unknown force.*

God is Spirit, **but He wants to reveal Himself to us.** *That's the reason for the Bible.* **That's the reason *why He came in person* ...why God the Son was *sent;* why the *"LOGOS"* became flesh.**

God does not desire to remain a mystery.

In the beginning of this book, I began by saying that **God is a very intensely passionate person** *with emotions just like ours.* In fact, *if we are indeed <u>His offspring</u>,* **we got our** *emotions from Him.* **We are His image and likeness.**

In other words, **He is a lot more like us than we think,** *because we are a lot more like Him than we think.*

We are wired to be like God.

No, I am not trying to reduce God into the image of fallen Man; into the image of fallen flesh, into a being who is ruled by His emotions, instead of controlling them. I am not reducing God to that, I am merely revealing TRUTH to you!

God wired us *to be like Him,* therefore **it is only logical to conclude that,** *in many ways,* **we sometimes act just like God and reflect His nature, who He is, when we tune into our hearts, to the core of our being!**

Based on this *reality,* the reality of what lies at the core of our being, I can say with confidence that, **just like us,** *God wants companionship.*

That's what happened in Genesis. God wanted someone *with whom He could share Himself. So He decided to* <u>make</u>, **to bring forth from within Himself, from the very core of His being, for Himself, such a companion.**

Before He did, however, He first created this whole world and everything in it.

In other words, **God, not desiring His heart of love for the companion He was about to bring forth, to remain a mystery, *expressed the attributes of His character in all of creation.***

I liken it to a man who prepares gifts in advance, before he goes to present himself to his bride to be. Or better yet, let's liken it to parents preparing a room and filling it with all kinds of surprises for their coming baby, *hoping that somehow that child would understand and grasp the love their parents have for them.*

Romans 1:20-21,

20 *"For since the creation of the world, His invisible attributes **are clearly seen, being understood** by the things that are made;*

*...**so that they are without excuse,***

21 **because, although they knew God, (they knew He existed, yet) they did not glorify Him as God, nor were thankful, but <u>became futile in their thoughts</u>.**

...and their foolish hearts became darkened."

It is their own futile thoughts <u>which darkened their hearts</u>.

They could have found THE TRUTH if they actually truly searched for it.

Psalm 19:1-4,

1 *"The heavens **declare** <u>the glory of God</u>, and the expanse of heavens **shows** <u>His handiwork.</u>*

2 *Day unto day **utters speech**, and night unto night **reveals knowledge**.*

3 *There is no speech, no language* (they communicate in silence; *nevertheless they are communicating,* and there is <u>no</u> people-group, <u>no</u> nation), ***where their voice is not heard.***

4 *Their reach has gone out throughout all the **earth*** (They have reached *the whole earth* with their silent but loud message),

*Their reach has gone out throughout all the earth and **their words to the ends of the world***"

Even throughout all generations *till the end of time!* **God's voice is everywhere!** Creation is trying *to tell us something.* There is *a hidden message in creation,* and all we have to do is **listen. God** is trying to communicate through creation. God is trying to ***reveal Himself,*** *His power, His person, His love,* through creation.

God is always *trying to **communicate*** with Man, trying to ***reveal Himself*** *to Man.*

He is trying to <u>reveal</u> His heart of love, HIS PASSION FOR MAN!

Let me ask you this: **What good is it for anyone to be the greatest person that has ever been, or ever will be, *if you cannot be known and appreciated and enjoyed <u>for who you really are</u>?***

As we read the creation account in Genesis you will notice this one thing to be true:

There is a whole lot of love and passion driving the creation of all things.

Creation is *God's love for Man* <u>on display</u>. It is God sending us ***a passionate love letter***.

Every time after creating something, God would stand back, evaluate, *and then enjoy what He just did.*

And the Bible says that,

*"God saw that **it was good**"* - Genesis 1:10, 12, 18, 21, 25.

1 Timothy 6:17 says,

*"God gives us **richly** all things to enjoy."*

Just think about it: When He created an apple, He didn't just leave it dull. He could have made it colorless and tasteless, without any smell, and dry as cork. But instead, He created it in all kinds of colors, shapes, and sizes.

He made it juicy with a sweet or sometimes tart taste, but always delicious. He could have left it at that. But no, He also gave it a distinct fragrance that is unmistakable and very likable.

Oh and that crunching sound it makes when you sink your teeth into it *makes it an unforgettable experience*...

Can you tell I like apples?

Ha… ha… ha…

Chapter 3

God Desires Companionship

God concluded every part of creation with the words,

"...it is good."

God put *His heart* into creation. There is nothing that was not put together **with considerable care** in all of creation. Everything God made came out **satisfactory.**

But what I want us to notice is that *the most momentous moment* in all of creation came right after God finally made Mankind.

The Scripture says in Genesis 1:27, 28, 31,

27 *"So God made Man in His own image; in the image of God He made him; male and female He made them*

28 *Then God **blessed** them...*

31 *Then God saw what He had made, **and indeed it was <u>very</u> good**."*

Now I know that God also *"**blessed**"* the rest of His creation as we can read in verse 22, but

Man was made as the culmination of all creation, and the reason for the preceding creation of all things, hence the term, *"**very good**"* was used in connection to the creation of Man, and in connection to the *"**blessing**"* God pronounced over Man.

Only after the creation of Man did God enter His rest.

That word *"**blessed**"* in the original language used here, is the word: BAW-RAK and *it is **an estimation of value*** term.

In connection with the *"**very good**"* announcement of God, this word *"**blessed**,"* this **estimation of value** term used here takes on new dimensions and a much deeper meaning.

Thus we find that this word BAW-RAK or *"**blessed**"* can also be defined as *an act of adoration* such as kneeling before, or *falling on your knees in wonder and amazement at the perfection of beauty.*

It is only used when a person is *entirely overwhelmed and in awe* of something.

It actually means that you are *so overwhelmed that you fall on your knees in adoration,* rejoicing in something.

It goes hand in hand with the phrase,

"...and indeed it was <u>very</u> good (exceptionally enjoyable)."

Zephaniah 3:17 says,

"He rejoices over us with gladness. He rests in His love. He is elated over you with singing!"

Only the creation **of Man, and nothing else,** *brought about that kind of reaction* from God. **Not the stars, not the earth, not the plants, not the animals. Nothing except the coming forth of Man** *brought about that kind of reaction* from God.

And let me tell you something: God is not on some ego trip. The reason for His rejoicing wasn't because He was so proud of His own abilities. *There is so much more to what was happening here than that!*

Everything God does has purpose. There is a reason for everything God does! And no, God wasn't kneeling and worshiping Man either. I don't want you to get the wrong picture here; **it is bad enough that people worship themselves and others.** *The last thing on earth I am interested in is promoting Man-worship.* (That's what the Naturalists and New-Agers and Humanists are into) *I'm not into that!*

There was a perfectly good reason for God's reaction. God rejoiced because

finally, here in front of Him, stood *the reality of His dream*. Finally, here in front of Him, stood a being *capable of being God's companion, capable of enjoying and sharing back and forth in the abundance of LOVE. Capable of not only giving God feedback, but enjoying God's feedback; deep calling unto and resonating with deep; back and forth enrichment; back and forth communication; back and forth appreciation, enjoyment, and satisfaction ...a constant, unending flow of friendship and fellowship and enjoyment of life together!*

In the gospel we are dealing with a most beautiful love-story!

In the desire for Man and the bringing forth of Man out of God's heart, we have the makings of the greatest of all love-affairs!

Finally, here in front of God, stood a being *capable of being God's COMPANION!*

What God **foreknew** was now *a reality.*

Again, that word *"foreknew"* has to do with the dream in your heart. Before that house you plan to build even gets started on, you have already seen it in your mind. In a way, you have already enjoyed it and lived in it. You have given it a lot of thought, so much so that you even know what it is going to look like when it is actually built. You can already taste what it's going to be like living in it. In that way you *"foreknew"* your house before it has even come into existence.

I am so glad that what God *foreknew* <u>became a reality</u>.

I am so glad God doesn't plan *and fail!*

Besides writing books, I sometimes paint with oils, or do some sculpting work on the side, just for the sheer pleasure of creating something.

Well, somehow my paintings and sculpting pieces never come out exactly like I had envisioned and pictured it in my mind. *Most of the time I still like it though.* It is a fantastic feeling to be able to enjoy your own handiwork, *but it can be quite frustrating when you are doing something and the thing just doesn't want to cooperate with you.*

Ha… ha… ha…

I also love chocolate cake. But when I try to make one myself, I inevitably get disappointed. The darn things just *never come out like the exquisite-looking, glossy picture on the box.*

Some of you may know what I am talking about…

God our Father, on the other hand, truly is a master-craftsman and an expert artist. After all *HE IS GOD, you know!*

Deuteronomy 32:3 & 4 says,

3 *"Ascribe greatness to our God, the Rock (the eternally immovable, unfailing, unchanging, steadfast One!)*

4 *"...**His work is perfect...**"*

Ephesians 1:11 says,

*"In Him we also have obtained an inheritance, **being pre-designed according to His purpose, <u>who works all things according to the counsel of His will</u>***..."

That means: **He doesn't plan and fail!**

When God created Adam, the man **was exactly** what God had in mind, *and God rejoiced in what Adam, in what <u>WE</u>, **you and I,** could now give Him.*

God has chosen to need us. That is what reveals our value. God has *chosen* us!
You are God's choice!

1 Corinthians 1:9,

*"God has **called us into the fellowship of** His Son, Jesus Christ."*

We have been called into the exact same fellowship that Jesus, the Son of God, enjoys with His Father.

God has an intense desire for us to encounter Him in an exceptionally high level of friendship, called: *"KOINONIA", or "Fellowship".*

"KOINONIA" or *"fellowship"* is a word that includes all the things we value in close relationship with one another: *friendship, communication, interaction, fun, companionship, partnership, camaraderie, intimacy, intercourse,* etc.

It is an awesome and wondrous thing to realize that we can fulfill something in God.

"Blasphemy!" Someone would say, "*God is perfect and needs nothing!*"

That is true. *He is GOD,* and *God* **is** *perfect.* It is true: **God needs nothing, BUT He has chosen to need us. He desires us because of LOVE.**

He *chooses* **to love us!**

He desires us!

1 John 4:8, *"**God** <u>is</u> **love**."*

Now you see, even in the natural, in order to *be* love, in order to *love* perfectly, *one must become vulnerable.*

Let me put it this way: **If God doesn't *need* us, if He doesn't desire us, He cannot truly *love* us.**

Even in the natural, love *needs* to be appreciated and to have *"KOINONIA"*.

Love also needs to be reciprocated, in order for there to be a *lasting intimate connection and fulfillment in relationship.*

You see; in relationship love has to have *feedback.* It cannot and will not be satisfied with anything less!

Love is more than mere emotions, but it *is extremely strong in its emotions.* Love *connects and feels* deeply! **It is totally engaged, there is no emotional disconnect!**

That's why God is a jealous God. His very name is JEALOUS! Not because He is petty and narcissistic, *but because there is no emotional disconnect in God!*

God is relentless in loving; **He loves us unconditionally, and in so doing, His love obliterates all competition! Love never gives up! It keeps on loving! Therefore, love never fails!**

God has never stopped loving us! **Nor will He ever! It is impossible! God's nature is LOVE!**

God is in love with YOU! *He is that much in love with YOU!*

God loves you unconditionally, and therefore that love will never fail! You can rely on it!

Grasping such everlasting love cannot but *quicken and cultivate a response of the same quality and kind in us!*

The apostle Paul said in Romans 2:4 that,

*"...***the goodness of God** (the love of God realized and grasped) *is exactly what leads us to* **repentance** (to *"METANOIA"*)...*"*

He gave birth to us **because He wanted us, *and He wants us still*! There can be no other conclusion! GOD IS IN LOVE** *WITH* **YOU!**

When I read the Genesis account of the creation of Man, *the conclusion is clear:*

GOD AND MAN WERE MEANT TO BE TOGETHER.

Genesis 1:26 & 27,

26 *"Then God said, 'Let Us* **make***'...*

(Note: Not *"BAW-RAW"* the usual word for **create,** but *"AW-SAW,"* **make – bring forth**)

*'Let Us **make** (Let Us bring forth) Man (from the depth of our being, from our heart) **according to Our image; <u>in</u> Our** (very) **likeness.'***

*'...**let them have dominion** over the fish of the sea, over the birds of the air, and over the cattle, over all the earth and over every creeping thing that creeps on the earth.'*

27 *So* **God made (brought forth) Man <u>in</u> His own image; <u>in</u> the image of God He made him;** *male and female He made them."*

Genesis 2:7,

"And the Lord God formed Man (our bodies only) *of the dust of the ground **and breathed into his nostrils the breath of life; and Man became a living being**."*

Our bodies might be fragile, created from the dust or clay, *but we are so much more than dust.* **You are** more than clay, *more than flesh and blood.* **You are a spirit-being.**

God took that lifeless clay body, *and breathed **you** into that body,* **from out of Himself; from out of His heart!** You are not from the earth, or earthly. *You are from above, **you come from God.*** **You have your origin in the eternal, invisible God: *in Him <u>who is Spirit</u>.*** He breathed you into your body **from the substance within Himself;** *from the very*

72

Spirit of God; <u>from the very "LOGOS!</u>" - John 1:1-4

Psalm 139:13 &14,

13 *"For You have formed **my inward parts*** (my spirit-being, the real me)*;*

*You have **covered <u>me</u>** in my mother's womb*

(That covering is not us; it is just the bodies we live in,)

14 *I will praise You, for <u>I</u> am fearfully and wonderfully made;"*

He is not talking about the body only, *but about* **YOU** *the real person on the inside.* **YOU** *are fearfully and wonderfully made.* You are not some *ugly, useless loser to be discarded as* **worthless.**

*"Marvelous are Your works, **And this my soul knows very well.**"*

Deep down, at the very core of your being, <u>you too</u>, *know these things to be true!*

We were conceived and created *in truth, truth was the substance we came from,* and we were brought forth *for truth* and *by The Truth Himself.* **Therefore we *were custom designed to respond to eternal TRUTH!***

Everything in you resonates when you hear these things *about your origin, identity, and true value ...about God, your true Father, your Daddy's love for you!*

The Spirit of God, the very Spirit of truth Himself *bears strong witness within your spirit* to these things.

Your spirit-man within you <u>knows these things to be true</u>! **Deep down in your spirit, you KNOW it to be true!**

"...and THIS my soul knows very well!"

I say again: You are more than just dust or clay. **You are a spirit-being conceived, created and brought forth out of the heart of God, out of God Himself, to be God's companion.**

You were designed to be inseparably linked to God.

When God breathed *His life* **into your nostrils, you became more than just flesh and blood!**

We were made *in* (according to - molded from - coined image - exact replica, literally *made out of HIM*) - **His image and likeness**.

He was not just the pattern, the mold, *but actually the <u>origin</u> of your being; <u>the very substance from which you came</u>*.

Man is more than just dust and clay. **Man is the only being conceived, created and brought forth from within God, from His very core, _to be His companion_. We are custom _designed_ to be inseparably linked to God. Man is a spirit-being MADE in God's image and likeness.**

Because Man was MADE _in God's image and likeness, it is only logical that he would act like God,_ especially before the Fall happened.

Adam was _a mirror image of God._ What was true about Adam was so <u>because</u> _it was first true about God._

If we look at Adam, before the Fall, _we can understand what was happening in the heart of God._

Genesis 2:18, 20, 22-24,

18 _"And the Lord God said, '**It is not good that man should be alone;** I will make him a helper **comparable to (compatible with) him.**'"_

It is a prophetic picture in which God reveals that _**it is not good, it is not preferable, for God to be alone. A helper comparable to and compatible with Him will be MADE; will be brought forth from within God ...just like Eve was taken out of Adam.**_

20 *"So Adam gave names to all cattle, to the birds of the air, and to every beast of the field.* **But for Adam there was not found a helper comparable to and compatible with him.***"*

Adam studied the animals to see what they were like, their little personalities and identity, and was able to accurately describe and define them, discovering their purpose. *But there was not found a helper comparable or suitable for him.*

You see, you can train a dog or a bird to be an excellent pet, *but that animal will never be a helper comparable or suitable for you.* **In the same way,** *God would not be satisfied with less than a helper comparable or suitable for Him.* **Man is that companion.**

Can you see with me *how everything that happens to Adam before the Fall* **carries a hidden message? It's so that we may discover a picture** *of what is in the heart of God towards us!* So we can see *how that He decided that it was no longer acceptable for Him to be alone,* how He longed for **companionship.**

Not because He was empty, but because of what He was enjoying within Himself.

That sweet **"fellowship"***, that joy, that life, that abundance, that enjoyment in the Holy Spirit, that enjoyment in the Son, in the "LOGOS",* **was so full and pleasurable and worth** *sharing that He felt compelled to reproduce Himself, and bring forth from within Himself, a companion, to lavish that LOVE, that FULLNESS upon.* A companion *from whom He could receive feedback and intelligent interaction and* **"KOINONIA" – quality "fellowship," quality friendship, and intimate companionship!** Whatever we read about Adam *prior to the Fall* reveals that.

Genesis Chapter 2 goes on to say,

22 *"Then the rib which the Lord God* **had taken from** *man He made into a woman, and He brought her to the man.*

23 *And Adam said, 'This is now bone of my bones and flesh of my flesh. She shall be called woman,* **because she was taken out of man**.*'"*

See, we were made *in*, literally **made out of** God's image and likeness **to be His companion.**

(Acts 17:28 *"For in Him we live and move and have our being."*)

The mystery of creation is no longer a mystery. **It is concealed in these Scriptures,** *but it is now revealed by the Spirit of God* <u>**for us to comprehend**</u>**!**

This <u>**reality**</u> **of** *our origin in God, of our oneness with Him,* **is a tremendous mystery**

that carries through all the way to Christ and the Church.

It is the dominant theme of Scripture.

When we look at Adam, **we see a reflection of that *connection, that absolute, inseparable association that exists between Man and God,* and therefore also between Christ and Man.**

Adam is a picture of God, and at the same time also a picture of Christ.

That close *connection* between God and Man *comes into its own, and is reflected to its fullest in the incarnation and work of redemption!*

When we look at Christ's *connection* and intimate love relationship with His Bride, *His body of believers who fully embrace their identification and union with Him ...when we look at we who are the "Church" (the "EKKLESIA"),* the ones who have _seen_ and _grasped_ and _understood_ and _embraced_ and _entered into_ and _enjoy_ the _reality_ of our identity and connection with the risen Christ, and with Father God Himself, that close connection between God and Man comes into it's own and is reflected to the fullest in the flesh; in this natural realm, in this natural dimension of existence!

23 *"And Adam said, 'This is now bone of my bones and flesh of my flesh. She shall be called woman, **because she was taken out of man.'"***

That phrase, *'This is **now** bone of my bones and flesh of my flesh…**because she was taken out of man'*** is so profound!

It is the prophetic Spirit of Christ, the prophetic voice of Jesus speaking to us and saying:

*"**YOU who come forth out of Me, out of My death, in My resurrection, born out of My faith, you are NOW inseparably linked to Me, bone of My bones and flesh of My flesh.**"*

*"…**You are now absolutely inseparable one with Me, totally connected to Me.**"*

We who embrace this reality of the love God has for us, we who embrace this reality that we come from Him, that we come out of Him, that He is our Daddy and our lover, we who embrace His faith, *we who believe and embrace these truths begin to experience that connection.*

We literally are the body of Christ Himself, where He comes to dwell, in all His wonderful fullness, in all His love.

It becomes more than just *some loose association* to us. His indwelling becomes a *reality,* His nearness our portion. It becomes a *connection,* an intimate, inseparable, uninterrupted *connection; close, intimate,* and *tangible!*

Marriage, just like it was in the beginning, between one man and one woman, as a natural reality, no matter how sacred, is only at best a picture of this spirit-reality we enjoy!

But what I want you to notice and see from this passage is just as Eve was *one with* Adam, *a part of Adam,* and *came out of Adam,* and *remained inseparably linked to Adam,* **we too come** *from* **Him,** *from* **God,** *from* **the** *"LOGOS",* from **Christ Jesus Himself.**

We *are one with Him, and we come out of Him.*

And we may have lost our way in our thinking, and practically, in all reality, in our experience, **but Christ came, and we were in Him. We are in Him, and we are one with Him, and we come out of Him, and, therefore, we also came out of Him in His resurrection from the dead.**

Exactly because that association; that eternal reality, that legal reality, could never be broken, or diminish over time!

It cannot be diminished by anything that happens in time!

We, you and I, the whole human race, *because of that legal, eternal, unbreakable association, legally were born anew in His resurrection.*

We were *quickened, made alive in relationship to God again, by His Spirit, legally and therefore literally, vitally, as a practical reality, in the resurrection of Jesus Christ.*

His resurrection *was and is the new birth of humanity.* His resurrection was *our* resurrection *to newness of life!*

All those who grasp and understand the reality of what happened there, *the reality that His death was our death, and the reality that His resurrection was our resurrection, because of that association*

...those of us who embrace these things as TRUTH, literally get overwhelmed by God's LOVE, and therefore embrace God our Father, as Daddy. And we experience the reality of that association, we experience that connection first hand.

According to Romans 15:13, there is,

"...joy and peace in believing."

It is *a faith thing* from start to finish!

It's <u>a conclusion</u> that leaves you with no other option than *the full embrace of its reality.*

It leaves you with no other option, but to believe! It is an embrace of reality itself! <u>*God's*</u> *reality!*

Everything else is unreal, a *"un-reality,"* an illusion and deception.

What God believes and knows to be true is the essence of REALITY! It is the essence of what is TRUTH! It is the essence of what is true and real!

What God believes and knows to be true ABOUT YOU <u>is</u> reality! It is the essence *of what is REAL!* Everything else is a lie!

You see, it is so much more than mind over matter.

It is so much more even *than just a mere mental acknowledgment, than just a mere mental acceptance of facts. It's more than just a mere choice* of the mind.

It is a faith thing from start to finish!

It's a heart thing; it's a falling in love thing!

Genesis 2:24,

*"Therefore a man shall leave his father and mother **and be joined** to his wife, **and they shall become one.**"*

This is also a great mystery!

Marriage in the natural, just like it was from the beginning between one man and one woman, as delightful and mysterious as that love may be, ***it is at best but a mere picture of the love-connection between God and us, and us and God, re-established in Christ, in His work on that cross, in His work of redemption, through which we fall in love with Him,** and **recognize** and **realize** and **live in the reality** of Him being our Daddy,** the God **who gave our spirits birth,** the One **from whom we came.** We **recognize** and **realize** and **live** in that **reality** of us being **His very own dear children, WHOM HE LOVES!**

*"**He who is joined to the Lord is one Spirit with Him**" - 1 Corinthians 6:17.*

But, before I get carried away, let's go back there to Genesis.

I want you to notice there that right from the very beginning; *God gave us everything we needed to be happy.* God created for Adam and Eve the most beautiful spot to live in, the Garden of Eden. They didn't even need clothes. They had nothing to be ashamed of because there was complete acceptance and transparency because of innocence in their relationship with God and one another.

There was no sin. They lived in harmony and total oneness with God and with one another. They had nothing to fear. Even the animals responded in positive submission to their loving masters.

Even cultivating and keeping the garden was a source of fulfillment and pleasure to them *because it originated out of their joy and enjoyment of one another and of life!*

That kind of abundance of life turns everything you do together into fun! Even work becomes fun! It is not what you are doing, per se. *It is who you are doing it with that makes all the difference in the world!*

Enjoyment was their portion!

I want you to notice with me that, because they were created to relate to God in the truest sense, _being together_ would not only be God's, but also their greatest fulfillment and enjoyment and reason for life itself.

God wants companionship, and it is mind blowing to realize that *Man is the only being that can fulfill that desire of God for intimacy.*

Until this revelation hit home, I never understood that *God could be hurt, grieved,*

or disappointed. Listen, *we are the only beings in all of creation with the capacity to do that.*

But before you get all condemned and sin-conscious, wondering if maybe you have disappointed and wounded God, let me tell you a secret: **God is not on a roller-coaster ride over you! He rests secure in His love for you!**

I am so glad that God is not ruled by disappointment, aren't you! I am so glad that God is not ruled by grief and bitterness and unforgiveness. I am so glad that God is not ruled by hurt and pain and fickle emotions. I am so glad that God rules His emotions with His heart. **I am so glad God's Spirit of Truth rules His heart.** *I am so glad that God has made His mind up concerning us!* You see, God cannot be moved. Love is unchanging and unconditional! Love is who He is; **He is love!** And in His love for us He gives and gives, and gives, and gives, and gives

...and positively anticipates

...and so it then also quickens a response of love from us ...a response, a love, that keeps growing, and growing, until it is of the same quality; until it matches His love for us!

We love Him, because He first loved us!

2 Corinthians 5:15,

"And He died for all, that those who live might no longer live for themselves, but for Him who died for them, and was raised again!"

Oh the depth of the love of God! Can you now see how God, **because of such enormous love and passion,** *can cry out with such disappointment and hurt after the Fall,*

"Adam, Adam, where are you?" - Genesis 3:9

...and yet still refuse to stop loving us, even though we broke His heart!

Herein lies the **good** *news:*

God may have been devastated at the fall of Man, *but no amount of disappointment or hurt could overrule His heart and mind and get Him to stop loving us. Otherwise Christ never would have come to rescue us ...and redemption would have been impossible!*

Chapter 4

God's Pursuit of Us

Of all the trees of the garden Adam and Eve could freely eat, **but from the knowledge of good and evil they had to stay away from.**

God told Adam *that they would die* **if they ate of the knowledge of good and evil.**

He didn't say **He would kill them** *if they ate of the knowledge of good and evil.*

No, God told Adam that *they would die* **if they ate from that tree, from that knowledge (the fruit, the knowledge itself, would poison them).**

He did not mean they would cease to exist; Adam lived a further 800 to 900 years or so.

But if they ate from that fruit, from the knowledge of good and evil, ***its poison would get into them***. *And* **because of its effect upon them *they would be separated from God and the life they were designed for*.**

Why did God even place this tree, *this option,* in the garden?

The only logical conclusion is that *He didn't have a bunch of mindless robots in mind when He made Man.* **He wanted Man to love and obey Him** *from the heart, by choice.*

That command to stay away from that tree, from that fruit, **from the knowledge of good and evil,** wasn't *an unfair test* by God either. It wasn't like putting candy in front of a child and telling that child not to eat it. There was so many other pieces of candy to enjoy in the garden, **the richness and the vastness of the knowledge of God is inexhaustible. There were so much to enjoy in their fellowship with God.**

Besides, Adam and Eve were adults. *In any adult relationship, there are natural boundaries created by their love for one another. Any married couple knows that. If you marry someone, there is an unspoken understanding that that person is going to wholly separate themselves unto you,* **no matter how many other people there are in the world.**

Adam and Eve had to deliberately choose to eat of that tree, of that fruit of the knowledge of good and evil, and bring death unto themselves.

The Snake (That cunning deceiver; the father of lies and deception) deceived Eve by getting her to question whether what God said was really true. Adam knew the truth. God spoke to *him*, not Eve, about that tree, about that fruit, **about the dangers of the knowledge of good and evil.**

Adam had the authority, he could have used *the truth of what God said* to stop Eve and resist the devil (that which is diabolical – from the Greek: diabolos, slanderer, to divide or separate, to cast down, to cause to fall), but he didn't.

Adam was not deceived about what God said. He knew full well what God said, but he did not correct Eve, ***because he also fell for the devil's trick. He embraced the lie*** and *began to question* **the truth** *of what God said.*

That poisonous serpent, the Devil, or Satan, sowed seeds of suspicion *and Adam allowed that suspicion towards God's motives to enter his heart and begin to germinate there.*

Adam began to question the TRUTH his heart already knew, he began to question God's heart and God's love and became suspicious towards God and began to question God's motives.

'What if this snake is telling the truth?'

'What if God actually does have ulterior motives?'

*'You know what? I'm truly beginning to wonder if what God said about that tree, about that fruit, **about the danger of that knowledge,** can be trusted.'*

It is easy to deceive an ignorant person. *But you see, an educated person has to deceive themselves through doubt and questioning and lying to themselves* in order to be deceived. **They essentially have to deceive themselves first, before any lie can stick.**

Therein lay Adam's guilt!

Adam deceived himself and swallowed the lie hook, line, and sinker. And in a moment of stupidity, he became rebellious towards God and decided to violate God's love by taking of that forbidden fruit of reasoning, of becoming a god unto yourself, of deciding for yourself what is good and what is evil and partaking of it and eating it.

But he didn't fully realize that he was **also violating something within himself** when he violated God's love.

He also didn't fully realize **the full extent of the poison** and of its *violation of everything pure and healthy and whole within him. He didn't fully realize what he was yielding himself and his spirit to; **that he was yielding himself and his spirit to the forces of death.***

Have you ever heard of a tree that bears fruit called, *"the knowledge of good and evil"?* Neither have I. I do not believe such a tree can be found. Although, I do not doubt that there probably was a literal tree in the garden, **but I want you to understand that that tree and its fruit represented something.**

You see, that tree and its fruit *is something outside of you and* **it represents a partaking of an outside force, an outside influence that now gets on the inside of you.**

It gets into your system and gets digested and becomes one with you.

I know what I am about to say may be controversial, but **it is not partaking of the fruit of the tree that brought about the Fall,** no, it is the Devil's manipulation and the embrace of the lie that opened up the door to Man's partaking of the knowledge of good and evil, and that is what the Fall is all about.

Thus **it is the embrace of the lie and deception that brought about the Fall,** not necessarily eating of the fruit of some natural tree naturally growing in a garden.

You see, that natural tree *was merely a prophetic picture pointing to and representing the Fall.* God said, *"In the day you eat of that tree you shall surely die!"*

Let me put it in another way to bring out the meaning of this prophetic picture and utterance by God. God was essentially letting Adam know that eating of that tree would be a sign to God and to Adam that something terrible *had already happened and was taking place inside of Adam.* **By the time he ate of that tree, *he would have already entered into deception and self-delusion, partaking of a knowledge other than God's, i.e. partaking of a lie.***

He would have already violated truth and entered into death, *into that which will cause a breakdown in the relationship, a separation between God and Man which God did not desire, but would have no control over once it happened.* Adam would bring it upon himself. He would bring it upon all of the rest of us.

That lie, that deception, that other knowledge, if embraced, will lead you into self-destruct mode. And then inevitably, partaking of that lie, of that deception, will surely lead you to partake of this tree, *even though God has warned you not to eat of it,* **it will lead you to partake of the knowledge of good and evil,** to basically become a god unto yourself, deciding for yourself what is right and what is wrong, what is good and what is evil.

It will lead you to the violation of your original design, and therefore ultimately to your destruction.

You see, eating the fruit of that tree had nothing to do with the Fall. *It was merely the outward sign prophetically pointing to the fact that the Fall had already happened.*

In Adam's partaking of that reasoning of the mind and of that other knowledge, that manipulation, that lie, that deception of the Devil; in Adam's one act of disobedience, **he unleashed deadly spiritual forces within himself,** *and thus exposed all future generations yet unborn, and all of creation to it.*

Eating of the fruit of that tree was merely the end result of that process.

Those deadly spiritual forces became like legal repercussions. *They became like cancer and left Man trapped and without escape!*

They had legal, *very practical, unavoidable, inescapable repercussions,* <u>just like a deadly virus or a cancer</u>. **And they cut him and everything under his authority off** *from God and the life it was designed for.*

He could not escape his violation, the serious repercussions, *the deadly poison* **of what he allowed in his heart and became bound by and subjected to in his thoughts and in his actions. It caused a very real separation.**

The Devil; the evil one, or ***that which is evil, powerfully and practically gained influence over Adam as well as over everything that previously was under Adam's authority, under Adam's influence, through Adam***.

Adam, without realizing the full extent of the consequences, the full extent of what he was doing, of what he was violating within himself, not knowing the full extent *of the consequences of that darkness, of what he embraced in his thinking,* **of what he was submitting himself to,** sold himself, his wife, all of Mankind still unborn, and the whole earth **in an illegal,** *but never the less, very powerful, practical and binding transaction to Satan's controlling influence and manipulation.*

The name, Satan, comes from the Greek word: satanos, which means **accusation,** as in adversary, or enemy. It speaks of opposing another in purpose and act, thus the term: *"accuser of the brethren"* And so the Devil also became the Satan or the Evil One. *It is all a reference the Fall.* **It refers to both that which caused or brought about the fall of Man, and the consequences or influence of the Fall upon the human race.**

So by the way, the word evil is the word Paneros in the Greek and it refers to something that causes, or is itself, full of hardships, labors, toil, annoyances, and frustrations.

Thus the tree of the knowledge of good and evil can also be referred to as the tree of deception, or the law tree, or the do-it-yourself tree, or the law of works and performance tree, because, the whole premise for eating of that tree was a lie. It promises that which is good, but in order to get to the good you also have to partake of Paneros: that which is full of hardships, labors, toil, annoyances, and frustrations.

The lie was that it promised life; it promised wisdom (that which is good and would aid you in life,) but instead it gave you death! *All you are left with is evil!*

It's a knowledge that is full of corruption; it is in and of itself SIN. It misses the point. It is in and of itself a poisonous evil. All you are left with is evil futility, *trying to become **who you already are,** and trying to achieve what you already possess; **what you have already been given as a gift!***

The term: SIN, is the Greek word, hamartia, and it means to miss, as in missing the point, or missing the mark; the target. It speaks of that which is without real merit.

Adam sold us **into bondage and slavery to evils' influence, manipulation, and rule** when he submitted to that temptation, to those forces of darkness, and rebelled against God *and became enslaved under sin and guilt.*

Adam literally brought it all *practically* under that spirit of manipulation, *that strong binding influence, that bondage.*

That separation from God and from everything Man was designed for *became Man's practical and long term experience and reality.*

The Law of sin and death, *that practical separation,* the law of sin and guilt and death **came into power and established its strong manipulation and rule, like a cancer, <u>like a virus</u> that took over the whole human race.**

The symptoms spread like a plague from generation to generation, *and the disease became firmly established and took charge.*

Separation came into law. It became *the new rule,* not the exception. It became <u>the new normal</u> *and evil reigned.*

The Bible says that *evil became the god of this world by that influence and manipulation and control of Adam and Eve and through them.*

They were trapped in the soulish realm, stuck in the natural-realm, *and reduced to a natural-minded dimension of life, a mere natural identity; an existence given over to the flesh.* In that state of mind *they made this* *world their god,* just as the Scriptures say they did in 2 Corinthians 4:4,

*"...**this world** (the attachment and dependence upon this world, this natural dimension, this natural existence, as if it has become your god, the worship of it) **has blinded the minds** <u>of them which believe not</u> **(those that question truth and lose sight of truth)**."*

In Ephesians 2:2 **that thing that now controls and manipulates Men's minds** through the law of sin and guilt and spiritual death is also called,

"...the prince of the power of the air, the spirit, who now works in the sons of disobedience."

That spirit, that prince of the power of the air, that **thing** that is in the minds of the sons of disobedience, that **thing** that is in them and has taken over their thinking, that **thing** we call Satan, was tempting Jesus with a similar, real temptation to the bondage Adam became subject to and reduced to, in Luke 4:5 & 6. It showed Jesus all the kingdoms of the world in a moment of time and it spoke to Jesus and said,

*"...I will give you all this power and authority **that has been turned over to me**, for I have **a right** to give it to whom I will."*

That **thing,** that **voice** wasn't lying; *otherwise it wouldn't have been a valid temptation.*

How did this **thing,** this **spirit,** this **thought-process** and **stronghold of thinking,** this **thing,** this **spiritual force,** this **thing,** this **spirit** which now controls and manipulates the sons of disobedience; *how did this **thing** first come into the power it now has?*

Through Adam.

It happened way back in the beginning.
Things started going wrong *way back in the garden.*

The Scripture also says in 1 John 5:19 that,

*"...the whole world **lies under the <u>sway</u> (under the influence and manipulation of)***

*...the **wicked one**."*

I want you to note though, that even though this **thing,** this **spirit force,** this **evil,** gained influence, power, and control, over mankind, by messing with Adam *in his thinking and in his heart, it was not actually a legal transaction,* although, for all intents and purposes, **practically,** it did come into power and rule.

It was actually *an <u>illegal</u> transaction; an <u>illegal</u> action!* **Why do I say that?**

Because Adam did not belong to himself.

Psalm 24:1 says,

*"The earth **is the Lord's** and the fullness thereof* ...*the whole world **and those** that dwell therein."*

God was and is, He remains the sole owner of it all! We are His! *The thief in his craftiness used ignorance and unbelief, suspicion, manipulation, and deception.* **He used a lie. He used lies and manipulation and deception, to set up an illegal transaction** *and to build up a stronghold for himself* **in Man's thinking,** *which he then also now* **maintains by force.**

That *power* the enemy has over people *became established* through one thing... Let me say it another way. **The *power* of Satan, the *power* of darkness lies in only one thing:**

MAN'S GUILT.

...**And the *influence* of that guilt, the power of it, the *strength* of that stronghold *within* Man is measured by one thing only:**

THE WEAKNESS OF THE FLESH.

The weakness of the flesh is first of all not a weakness *in our body*. It has nothing to do

with the body. *The body is but a glove that does as the soul directs.*

The weakness of the flesh is A WEAKNESS IN OUR THINKING that ties us to a mere natural mindset, a natural-minded existence, a fleshly existence in separation from God.

It is that *false thinking* that came about in the Fall.

That false thinking is **established and then reinforced,** *through guilt and manipulation and sin-consciousness,* **through our cooperation.**

You see; it all came into power *because of that initial* <u>cooperation</u>. *That lie that was introduced and embraced* way back in the Fall, *that very deception and wrong mindset and flawed belief-system* <u>that was embraced</u> *became established.*

And the enemy uses that very stronghold of deception *to maintain his power and his strong rule over Man.*

The enemy built up a stronghold for himself *in Man's thinking which he now maintains* <u>*by force*</u>.

But I have news for you *that will liberate you:* The enemy is nothing but *a thief.* He is not *the strong man he claims to be!* The so called power that he has over people *is weak!*

He used <u>lies</u> and <u>manipulation</u> and <u>deception</u> *to set up that illegal transaction, to set up that power.*

He used *a legally weak transaction to build up his stronghold.*

It is an *illegal transaction and thus it is a weak, illegal stronghold.*

And I want you to know that *no matter how long a thief has something in his possession,* <u>his claims of ownership are weak</u> because *the minute he is discovered and the deception of his plot is exposed by the truth,* he has to return what was stolen.

In the light of eternal truth, the lie of the enemy, and the guilt driven manipulation and sin-consciousness he uses to keep us in death, to keep us separated from God, and to manipulate us with, and to have power and control over us, and to have his way with us ...it all loses its power and affect upon us, in the light of that eternal truth.

I thank God for what Jesus said in John 8:32,

He said, *"You shall know the truth, and the truth shall make you free!"*

He also said in John 12:31, *"**Now** shall the prince of this world be <u>**cast out**</u>!"*

And in Luke 10:18 He said, *"**I saw Satan fall** like lightning from heaven."*

He spoke all this **in relation to us understanding the successful work of redemption He was about to accomplish!**

But let us get back to what happened in Genesis. There was nothing Adam and Eve could do to rescue themselves *from that strong deception and that manipulation, or the rule of sin, and of the enemy, that came about through it, nor the damage that was done by it.*

They could not escape what they were snared in and ruled by. They could not simply restore themselves back to God. The separation was complete. *It became a permanent condition **because they remained trapped in a natural dimension through their soul-realm thinking and wrong mindset. They were trapped** through that stronghold set up and built by the enemy within them.*

Even if they could re-discover the truth, *there still remained the matter of **legality, of <u>real and binding guilt</u> in their hearts and minds.***

*There still remained **legitimate guilt** that could not merely be overlooked.*

There had to be some kind of legal transaction between them and God that would, <u>in their minds</u>, legally and practically remove their guilt and sin-consciousness, and restore to them, in their hearts, what they had lost. It had to restore to them that identity and righteousness, that innocence they once enjoyed, in the beginning, in the presence of God, in their friendship with God.

You see the Fall *happened to us, because it happened in our thinking, in our minds,* and therefore it happened in our hearts.

Legally, actually, practically, it became a binding reality in our spirits and lives.

But I thank God that *the Fall never happened to God. God never fell; we did.* We got lost and confused, but God never lost His way.

You see; He made up His mind about us long before time began. He never lost track of the truth. God never fell from His love either. He never lost track of our value or our worth! *He never stopped loving us! God never fell; we did!*

God's mind is made up about YOU! *He knows who you truly are,* and He made up His mind. He is never going to stop loving you; *the real you, MADE in His image and likeness,* no matter how confused and lost you may be! That's why He refuses to give up on *you!*

So, even though nothing had changed concerning Him and us, and His desire for us to be His companions, as far as the eternal, unchanging God was concerned, He knew and understood that within ourselves, we lost something precious. We lost our INNOCENCE. It became a binding reality to us. We could not just get back that innocence, by ignoring sin and guilt.

God felt for us, and with us, *that pain of separation,* and He knew that *pure LOVE would have to take the initiative and intervene* in a legal, *strong, binding way,* just like a father would have to do *when trying to free a son* who got caught up *in some binding illegal activity and consequential police matter.* Even God cannot just ignore *a legal matter,* a *binding* matter, *a binding reality.*

I am so glad that, even though it was an illegal action, <u>*and only legally binding in our minds and hearts,*</u> *and not an actual legal reality in God's mind and heart,* I am so glad that God could not, *and did not,* just ignore our binding reality. He chose not to ignore *the practical reality we lived in!*

He did not *leave us in our bondage.* He came to deal with it *and set us free* and restore, as a practical reality for us, as a legal, binding reality for us, *that place we originally had in Him. That place we never actually lost as far as He was concerned!*

You see, and I want you to get this clearly: **Even though it is an illegitimate matter** *as far as God is concerned,* **God could not just violate,** *in our minds and our hearts,* **what was legally done!**

What we consider to be legal *is in all practicality legally binding upon us.* **It is** *a practical reality!* **He couldn't just** *forgive* **Man's sin,** *exactly because, in our minds and our hearts, in our incomplete, inaccurate, even warped knowledge of Him, He is known by us as "JUDGE of all the earth".*

In the natural, a judge would be considered unrighteous if he just ignored a man's sin and forgave him anyway.

No, God had to come and deal with the matter in a legal way, *a binding manner.* **It was clear that only God could do something about the situation** *and He had to do it by satisfying all the legal terms required in man's mind and heart. He had to cleanse our conscience.*

God could have just given us our punishment of death and killed us, *but in His mind and heart* <u>that was not an option</u>.

I say again: <u>It was not an option</u>! How could He do such a thing; how could He just give us our punishment of death and kill us? He couldn't! *We were His own dear children.*

There was no way He was about to start over with another creation *when He still loved us SO MUCH!*

He had to demonstrate the love He still has for us in no uncertain terms!

But let's get back to Genesis quickly. You see, He could have destroyed Adam and Eve. ***But He loved them** and gave them a promise: one day, through **the Seed** (not many seeds, but the one Seed) of the woman **(through Jesus and our absolutely legal, unbreakable, eternal association with Him),** **He was going to rescue us and set us free from Satan himself and his forces of darkness, from the dominion of <u>that virus</u>, that evil one, <u>that thing that invaded us</u>.***

God gave Adam and Eve that promise because He is a good God, *because He loves us.*

Did you know that He put them out of the garden <u>*because of love*</u>.

"…lest they eat also of the tree of life and remain in that fallen state forever." - Genesis 3:22.

God never stopped loving us! He always kept a way open for our return to the garden. That secret way, that gate to the entrance of the garden, that hidden passage way, that gives access to the tree of life, was guarded by two Cherubim with flaming swords in their hands. I suggest to you that it is the spirits of wisdom and revelation in the knowledge of Him. **I thank God that redemption in Christ Jesus is not an afterthought, a plan B. No, it is a total restoration and continuation of plan A! A restoration of TRUTH, of REALITY, of our LEGAL and PRACTICAL place in Him.**

Even in the Old Testament Scriptures the grace of God can still be seen. Even there His love for us is still apparent!

Every one of God's Names revealed to His people Israel in the Old Covenant *represents a manifestation of who He is in His love towards His covenant people; towards us. We are the real covenant people of God.*

God chose Israel to be the people through whom *the Seed* of the woman would come *that would bless the whole world*. **That is the only reason why they were prophetically called, *His people.***

They were of prophetic significance **and would only be God's people <u>as a nation</u>** *until the Messiah would come.*

*Once the Messiah came, then **they as a nation would no longer be God's only and special people,** but now they would have to join the rest of the world **as individuals,** and together, **from every tribe and tongue and nation (including the Jews),** all those individuals who believe on the Messiah and His work of redemption would then be His **new royal priesthood,** His **new holy nation,** a peculiar people, set apart unto Him, on the earth,*

…aliens and sojourners …in the world, but not of the world …the very children of God **restored to their original identity as sons of God.** *They would be **the real people of God,** restored to their true Father, restored to that original image and likeness **already within them!***

Israel became God's chosen people, God's chosen nation, exclusively set apart, *so that all the nations of the world would be blessed through them.*

But now God has chosen us *believers,* **set apart by faith** *through understanding of the gospel,* **to be His** *"Church",* **a** *new* **holy nation,** *a new* **special people of faith,** *exclusively set apart unto Him.*

So that now Israel can be blessed in return through us, through us making the gospel

known to them, and through our intimate
relationship with God, as father; as Daddy.

And in that way, in God's plan, not just the
Jews, **but all the nations _together_** will be
blessed **through the gospel**.

That is exactly how God's election works, *not*
to exclude, but to **include.**

God selects or elects one *through which* **to**
bless the rest!

He always has more than the individual or the
one nation in mind in election. His choice is to
bless everyone, **so He chooses one** through
whom to bless everyone. *Because really;*
everyone is included in His election. **It seems**
like He excludes, *but it is only in order to*
include!

God's purpose has always been, and still
is, to include and reconcile the whole world
to Himself!

There are literally dozens of Scriptures and
parables in the Old Covenant that liken Israel
to a lover whoring around and disappointing
God as her companion. It was all pointing to
the fact that even though they as a nation and
a people were elected for a purpose, **they**
were not truly His people. _And that they_
too, like all the rest of the nations have
been under the effects of the Fall and that
God was therefore going to have to reject them

as a nation from being His exclusive people **when the Messiah came, *because they too, just like the rest of the world, would have to INDIVIDUALLY enter into the kingdom of God.***

They would have to enter into the "Church" and become His own special people, the elect of God, <u>individually</u>, THROUGH FAITH, <u>by embracing and believing the truth</u> of the gospel; the truth revealed and restored in Christ Jesus, the Messiah, in His work of redemption.

Isaiah 5:1-7 talks about Israel's disappointing and whoring ways as lover and companion to God,

1 *"Now let me sing to my Well-beloved. A song of my Beloved regarding His vineyard;*

My Well-beloved has a vineyard on a very fruitful hill.

2 *He dug it up and cleared out its stones, and planted it with the choicest vine. He built a tower in its midst, and also made a wine press in it;* **so He expected it to bring forth good grapes, but it brought forth wild grapes**.

3 *And now, O inhabitants of Jerusalem and men of Judah; Judge, please, between Me and My vineyard.*

4 *What more could have been done to My vineyard that I had not done in it?*

Why then, when I expected it to bring forth good grapes did it bring forth wild grapes?

7 *For the vineyard of the Lord of hosts is the house of Israel and the men of Judah are His pleasant plants.*

He looked for justice, but behold, oppression; For righteousness, but behold, weeping."

As His chosen people, as His prophetic people, for years and years He reached out to the nation of Israel, *but they refused Him.*

This was all one big prophetic picture indicating the state of the fallen human race and pointing to the Messiah to come through them as a people.

It is exactly because of this heritage, being children of Abraham who was God's friend, and being chosen as a people to bring in the Messiah, *and because Jesus has a body that comes from them ...it is exactly because of that, that God has a special place in His heart for the Jews **still**. What I mean is that **He desires for them**, through whom the Messiah came, **to understand His heart and to embrace their salvation; to embrace the truth as it is revealed and restored to us in Jesus.***

This gospel was meant for all the nations, *for all people individually, but especially for them who had a particularly special part to play in the coming and incarnation of Jesus.*

Yet to this very day a large portion of them still reject Him, just like they did in Jesus' day.

Can you just see His passion for them in this next verse?

Matthew 23:37,

"O Jerusalem, Jerusalem, the one who kills the prophets, and stones those who are sent to her!

How often I wanted to gather your children together, as a hen gathers her chicks under her wings, but you were not willing!"

We do have God's promise and challenge, though, not to give up on these people *whom He has such a special place in His heart for,* because He prophesied through Paul in Romans 11:25 that *their eyes will eventually be opened to see the truth and understand the gospel.*

*Paul clearly indicated that **God is going to use the "Church", His new holy nation, His own special people of faith, us, the believers, to reach them and help them***

***come to the knowledge of salvation and of
the truth.***

But it was not just Israel who rejected God.
They were just a prophetic picture of the rest.
It was obvious that mankind *as a whole* **just
became progressively worse and needed
Jesus the Savior to come.**

Psalm 8:4,

*"What is Man that You are mindful of him, and
the Son of Man that You bother with him,
God?"*

Isaiah 53:6,

*"All we like sheep have gone astray; we have
turned, every one, to his own way;"*

Romans 3:9-12 & 23,

*"Are we any better than they? No, not at all,
for we are all under sin's dominion. All have
sinned and fall short of the glory of God.*

There is none righteous, no not one; ***there is
none who understands;*** *there is none who
seeks after God.*

They have all gone out of the way; ***they have
together become unprofitable.****"*

Let me tell you something, all you have to do is
read your history books. Or even still today, all

you have to do is watch the news on television or open a newspaper and it becomes obvious: **The disease that destroys humanity had fully taken root, and the symptoms abounded.**

Even until now, it still abounds within the ignorant and unbelieving.

Because of all these very many offenses over time, it was like *"the accuser of the brethren,"* Satan himself, was crying out louder and louder, trying to get God's attention. Trying to mock God and degrade humankind all together by saying, *'Hey GOD! Humanity **doesn't deserve** Your love.'*

You see, what he didn't understand and still does not fully comprehend about God is that, *even though God **has every right** to destroy us, **He has made His mind up to love us and rescue us and deliver us from the devil, or Satan, from this <u>thing</u>, the evil one, the wicked one** ...<u>because of our eternal association in Christ Jesus</u>.*

God has never stopped loving us, *because He has forever made up His mind to do so!*

He loves us, *even still* today!

It has always been God trying to win our favor, not the other way around.

Companionship and intimacy *is what God wants from us.* Intimacy with God is also *what we need* **to be fulfilled.**

That is what is behind the death of Jesus on our behalf.

We were all *doomed to perish.* **We disgraced God. We violated His trust and insulted His goodness and kindness towards us.** In *ignorance and self-deception* **we walked all over His love. We came under Satan's influence and dominion in the Fall and were all living in a hell of our own making. We built it ourselves! We built it together with Satan! We were all hell bound! We were all lake of fire bound!**

Let's talk about hell and the lake of fire for a second. Oh yes, you better believe that hell and the lake of fire is so much more than just a miserable life of our own making and Satan's making **in the here and now on planet earth.** *It is a real place, just like heaven is a real place. No, it's not a place, like in relating to a natural place. You can't look at it as a natural place or even as a place.* **It's a dynamic which exists in spirit dimension. It's a spiritual dynamic, not a physical place!**

Most people want to conveniently forget about these spirit dimension realities of hell and of the lake of fire, BUT if we do that, we might as well forget about the concept and dynamic and *reality of heaven as well! These realities are just as real, they exist, just as heaven and Earth exists. Earth exists in a natural dimension, while heaven exists in a spirit dimension. The same Bible that teaches us about Heaven's reality, that it does exist, **also teaches us** about the reality of hell and of the lake of fire. These are all dynamics that exist in spirit dimension!*

*Jesus spoke quite a bit about hell; almost just as much as He spoke about heaven, **and He had quite a bit to say about the subject.***

*We do however need to thoroughly grasp and comprehend what exactly Jesus was referring to when He brought up that concept and that word: "Hell," **because there are several Greek words used for the word: "Hell," and every one of those different words had to do with different concepts that greatly differ from each other.** We must also remember that whichever specific word and concept Jesus brought up in conversation with any group of people of His day, held an exact meaning to that specific audience at the time.*

But I did not write this book to talk about Sheol, Gehenna, Hades, Tartarus, the Abyss, the Pit, outer darkness, or the Lake-Of-Fire. I want us to notice, and to <u>focus on</u> the fact that Jesus spoke <u>much more</u> about our Father's LOVE for us <u>than about</u>

heaven, hell, or any other such spiritual dynamic or reality!

Love's <u>reality</u> *far supersedes that of Hell's.*

God's *"perfect LOVE..."* *"...casts out <u>all fear!</u>"*

Listen, *hell was not created for us!* Hell is a dynamic, a reality reserved for Satan and his angels.

Did you know that people *<u>live in a hell of their own making</u>, and that reality even extends into their future as a dynamic and experience of their own making?*

God is not <u>*sending*</u> anyone to a hell of His making!

God <u>*doesn't want*</u> us to end up in a hell of our own making, *or join the devil in any future reality of hell!*

God does not desire <u>*that any* of us</u> should perish!

1 Timothy 2:4,

"God desires all Men (all mankind; every single individual) *to be saved and to come to* (or to be saved by coming to) *the knowledge of the truth."*

If we perish and end up in some future hell of our own making, it will be because of stubborn unbelief, or refusal to believe. *It will be the inevitable result of a rotten attitude and a rejection of love and eternal truth.*

It will not be by God's hand, but by our own doing, because, just like the prodigal son's brother, and just like the Pharisees of Jesus' day, our reality is our own, it's of our own making; we judge <u>ourselves</u> unworthy of eternal life!

But, God loves us *so much, He loves you so much that He is not about to give up on you!*

God has not given up on a single person on the face of the earth!

Love never quits trying to reach the ones they love!

1 John 5:11 & 12,

11 *"God has given us eternal life, and this life is in His Son.*

12 *He who has the Son has life*; He who does not have the Son of God *does not have life."*

How do you get the Son?

I want you to read it carefully and realize with me that *the issue is not getting the Son.* ***The real issue is UNDERSTANDING THAT ETERNAL LIFE <u>that God has given us</u> and <u>that was manifested</u> and <u>then redeemed and restored to us</u> in the Son's work of redemption.***

The issue was and always will be: UNDERSTANDING!

John 17:3

"And this is eternal life: ***That you may <u>know</u> the only true God,*** *and Jesus Christ whom He has sent!"*

When you grasp your Father's love for you, and get caught up in that intimate relationship; that love affair, it determines not just your present reality, but all future reality!

That is why Hell is a non-issue for anyone who embraces the fullness of redemption!

Listen, that work of redemption was a success!

Once we believe these things and EMBRACE them, Jesus and the Father will manifest themselves in us and to us, and come and make their home in us, by that resurrected Spirit of Christ, the Spirit of Truth, who proceeds from both the Father

and the Son, *and who comes to make these things a reality in us!* He comes to persuade us of TRUTH, and then Christ comes and lives in our hearts BY THAT TRUTH WE EMBRACE; BY THAT FAITH.

As I said before, *it's A FAITH THING from beginning to end!* **As we fully embrace the faith of God and believe these things *and become persuaded in them and by them, we begin to experience God in reality!*** That is what Jesus Himself said in John 14, 15, 16, and 17.

John 14:20,

"In that day you will know that I am in My Father, and you in Me, and I in you!"

You see, at one time we were all without hope and without God in the world. We were alive, but we had no LIFE. We lived in separation from God, in separation from Life Himself. We lived in death. In ourselves, there was nothing we could do about it. **As long as the law of sin and death still legally stood against us, *in our minds and in our hearts,* there could be no reconciliation between us and God.**

BUT God in His goodness, *because of the great love with which He loved us, and with which He loves us still,* sent Jesus. God put it all on the line! He laid Himself bare, and He made His heart fully known, in a very clear way, in no uncertain terms.

**Yes, it took *the extravagant love of God* ...
*the enormous sacrifice of Christ;***

***...It took God, at enormous personal cost,
to demonstrate His love for us* ...and by so
doing, *to redeem and rescue* our minds and
our hearts out of darkness!**

John 3:16,

*"For God **so exceedingly much loved the
world** (everybody, all of us) *that He sent the
Son* (the authentic, original One; begotten only
of God; our blueprint; the only Blueprint Son
and Savior), *Jesus Christ, **that we through
Him, through that work of redemption and
the truth revealed in Him, might be saved.***"*

Romans 5:8,

*"God demonstrated **His own love TOWARDS
US,***

*...**in this;***

*...**while we were still sinners**, Christ died for
us."*

**You see, if I have offended my friend, it is
up to that friend, *in their own initiative,* to
forgive my transgression. *In my mind and
heart,* I cannot justify just merely ignoring
the offense. In fact, legally, righteously, it
has to be on my friends own initiative that
they *choose* to forgive me. *It is up to them***

to forgive me. It is only based on their initiative to forgive me that I find the legal grounds to embrace, <u>in my mind and in my heart</u>, that forgiveness <u>and forgive myself</u>, before I can even continue in the friendship without any guilt or shame or embarrassment and self-condemnation of any sort.

This is precisely what God did!

Ephesians 2:4 & 5 says,

4 *"But God, <u>who is rich in mercy</u>, because of His <u>great love</u> with which He loved <u>us</u>,*

5 *even when we were dead in our trespasses, <u>made us alive together with Christ</u>* (by grace you have been saved.)*"*

We really must stop focusing on our unworthiness and begin *to focus on God's grace, on His goodness. He made us <u>worthy</u>.*

Isaiah 53:5 says,

"He (Christ) *was wounded <u>for OUR</u> transgressions, bruised <u>for OUR</u> iniquities.*

The chastisement <u>for our peace</u> was upon Him..."

Ephesians 1:6 says, *"God made us <u>accepted</u> in the Beloved."*

Ephesians 2:8 continues,

*"**By grace** are you saved, through faith **(through God's faith becoming our faith),** and that, not of yourself, **it is the gift of God.**"*

And Colossians 2:13-15 says,

13 *"**And you, being dead in your trespasses (in other words, still being under that law of sin and death and its enslavement; yes you) He made alive together with Him,***

*…**having forgiven** you **all** trespasses…"*

How did He do it?

14 *"**He wiped out the handwriting of requirements that was against us, which was contrary to us**…"*

He is talking about *"**the law of our minds and hearts**", "**the knowledge of good and evil**", "**our own legalistic thinking**", "**that accusation and condemnation**"*

…that very sin we know and feel we have committed against Him.

He is talking about *"**that lie and deception from the enemy we have embraced**"* and the obligations which we came up with, and tried to live up to, *to try and undo our guilt and win God's favor,* but couldn't fulfill in ourselves;

He is talking about *"…**that religion we have embraced**" and the guilt and condemnation because of it all that we couldn't free our minds and hearts* from.

*"…**He has taken it out of the way**,"*
*"...**having nailed it to the cross**."*

He set us free from the power which the law of sin and death had over our lives ***by this mighty display of His love.***

<u>And this is a totally legal action because of that legal, eternal, valid association in Him.</u>

15 *"Having **disarmed** principalities and powers, **He made a public spectacle of them, triumphing over them in it**."*

He legally reconciled us. His *love* rescued us! He stripped the enemy of his power! *The enemy's lies and deception and guilt-driven manipulation lost its authority!*

That is fantastic news. That's *the Gospel. The Gospel* by its own definition means **GOOD NEWS!**

God established the New Covenant *in such a way that we cannot mess it up!*

He established it, not with us, *but with our representative, Jesus Christ.*

124

Not between us and Him *so we can fail again in upholding our end of it, NO!*

He established **the New Covenant. He actually came and He** **re-established** **that original eternal Covenant made between Himself and the Son.**

This is absolutely to OUR benefit. **He opened up a new and living way for us. New to us, new in time, but not new to Him!**

Now He is pleading with us to simply *be* **reconciled on that basis, to come and enjoy our reconciliation,** *to come and embrace our Daddy again,* **to come and enjoy the bliss** *of innocence and friendship* **again!**

2 Corinthians 5:18-21 states that,

18 *"God* **has** *reconcil*__ed__ *us (past tense) to Himself through Jesus Christ,*

19 **God was in Christ; (He came in person) reconciling** **the world** **to Himself;**

…**not imputing their trespasses to them.**

20 *Therefore we are ambassadors for Christ,* *as though God were pleading through us;*

…**we implore you** **on Christ's behalf,** **be** **reconciled to God,**

21 *For He made Him (Jesus) who knew no sin to be sin for us;*

...**_that in Him (in His work of redemption) we might become (not slowly over time, but instantly, through faith, be restored to) the righteousness of God._**"

God made a legal exchange. He made Jesus to become sin with our sinfulness, and He nailed that Sin, that sinfulness to the cross, in Jesus, **so that we might become righteous with His righteousness,** *with that original righteousness.*

Verse 17 says,

17 "**_Therefore_ (Based on the right conclusion** – *the conclusion mentioned earlier in verse 14*)..."

Based on that conclusion, based on God's conclusion, based on the fact that *God concluded that everyone is in Christ and that everyone died in Christ, based on that conclusion, he says, Verse 14,*

14 "*If one died for all, then all died!*"

Or, "*Since One died for all, therefore all died!*"

...**based on _that_ conclusion then, he says,**

17 "*...if therefore anyone is in Christ,*"

Or, *"...**since therefore** everyone is in Christ (**that person that is in Christ <u>therefore</u>, as <u>God Himself</u> has concluded**);"*

Paul says, *that person,*

*"...**he <u>is</u> a new creation;"***

*"...old things **have** pass<u>ed</u> away (there in Christ's death) ...behold, **<u>all</u> things <u>have</u> <u>become</u> new."***

In Colossians 1:12-14 Paul says,

12 *"**God the Father <u>has qualified us</u> to be partakers of the inheritance** of the saints **<u>in</u> <u>the light</u>** (**In the light of truth, *or by* revelation into the truth,** we become saints, or set apart ones, or purified ones; we become partakers of that inheritance **when we embrace God's light; when we believe God's truth**).*

13 **He <u>has</u> deliver<u>ed</u> us from the power of darkness** *(or ignorance and deception);*

*...**and translat<u>ed</u> us** into the kingdom of (Christ) the Son **of His love,***

14 *In Him **we <u>have</u> redemption** through His blood, (we <u>have</u>) the forgiveness of sins **(already)."***

In the *Vines Expository Dictionary of New Testament Words*, the word *"**redemption**"* means **the price was paid.** It means **to purchase; to buy out.** It speaks of **releasing on receipt of ransom, to release by paying a ransom price, to redeem.** It is especially used in *the purchasing of a slave with a view to his freedom,* **setting at liberty.**

The Scriptures do not say to whom the price was paid.

The word redemption is used *to describe, not only the release from the consequences of the transgressions,* **but from the actual transgressions themselves.**

It is also used in the middle voice,

...**to buy up for oneself.**

It also refers to *buying up* **an opportunity** or **making the most of every opportunity** and *turning it* **to the best advantage** *since it cannot be recalled if missed.*

I want you to understand that **God didn't need to come to negotiate with Satan for your release. God had no dealings with the devil. He owed Satan nothing.** *He fully understood that to enter into a negotiation with Satan would cost Him His throne. Satan would not have been satisfied with anything less.*

Besides, you don't need to negotiate **with a thief.** *It doesn't matter how long something has been in the thief's possession,* **it does not** *belong to him, <u>and never will</u>.* No, God didn't come and bargain with Satan, *He didn't need to.*

God came to negotiate with us.

If He was trying to buy back a used up humanity from Satan, *He would have tried to pay the lowest possible bargain price.* But no, *He paid the highest price. He placed the highest value upon our lives, upon us, upon YOU,* because He wasn't negotiating a transaction with Satan, *He was dealing with us.*

He had to cancel our debt in order to rescue <u>our minds and hearts</u>.

His transaction had to convince us <u>of our worth and of our value to Him still</u>!

In that negotiation, in that transaction on that cross, He, without even dealing with Satan directly, *totally defeated Satan (that serpent of old that became a fierce unbeatable dragon in our minds) and He (God) stripped him of all his authority <u>by disarming and exposing him, making a public spectacle of his lies and deception</u>.*

In revealing the truth of His love for us, God embarrassed Satan publicly and took away what Satan used as leverage to maintain power over us *when He (God) canceled our debt, and thus proved to us that we are of the highest value to Him still.*

And by so doing, He canceled out the fall and all its consequences, and released us from the debt **of our minds and hearts,** *the debt He* **now proved** *we never really owed.*

You see, IN TIME, God had to come and through that act on the cross, pay our debt, and thus forgive us. <u>IN TIME</u>, IN CHRIST, He dealt so thoroughly with that debt of sin that He could remove it totally from His own mind and never even remember it again.

There are lots of Scriptures that declare that God has, in Christ, forgiven us and *"removed our sins from us as far as the east is from the west,"* and that, *"our sins and lawless deeds He will remember no more."*

"In Him we <u>have</u> redemption, the forgiveness of our sins."

Thus, <u>IN TIME</u>, God forgave us, and proved to us our forgiveness.

But IN ETERNITY, IN THE ETERNAL AGES PAST, God already forgave us before there ever was a redemption. In fact, He forgave us even before the Fall, even before creation.

From that realm outside of time, from the realm of ETERNITY, *He saw the end from the beginning and chose not to hold anything against us.* **Thus, in His mind and heart, the Lamb (Christ Jesus) was slain,** *from before the foundations of the earth already.*

God never lost track of the truth about us. We may have been deceived, we may have fallen away from truth and from Him, we may have fallen into sin and into darkness, BUT HE NEVER DID.

It is an ETERNAL REALITY that God never stopped loving us and *He overlooked the times of ignorance.*

It is an ETERNAL REALITY that *He did not hold our trespasses against us*

...and thus **in His own heart, He never actually needed to forgive us of anything.**

The price He paid had to be <u>to us</u> *...so that it could be seen and received and embraced by us, as final confirmation of His love* <u>for us</u> *...so as to fully convince* <u>us</u> *of our worth and our value to Him* <u>still</u> *in spite of the Fall.* **(He had to rescue** *our minds and hearts* **from strongholds of darkness,** *from lies and deception and ignorance and sin and guilt and condemnation!***)**

AND HE DID SO, IN THE WORK OF REDEMPTION.

In redemption, God gave us *a time in which something is seasonable*, i.e. *a seasonable opportunity* **to believe in His love,** *to* **embrace** *the work of salvation,* **and** **be** **reconciled to Him!**

Allow me to expand on these radical thoughts about God *not coming to bargain or negotiate with Satan,* **but with us,** and about God, *"not imputing our trespasses to us,"* ...about Him coming in person, *not to deal with any legal reality in His own mind and heart,* **but to undo the binding reality of our minds and hearts.**

He came **to cancel our debt that exists in our minds and hearts in order to rescue** **our** **minds and hearts**.

I am repeating myself, so you can get it **cemented and established** *in your own heart and mind,* because, for so terribly long, humanity as a whole, *and we ourselves also, for most of our lives* **have had such an inaccurate, warped view of God,** that it might be hard for some of you **to accept** *what I am saying, or even* **to grasp it** *and try and hold on to it and retain it.*

But allow God to create *a new mindset in you,* **a new way of thinking**, *a new wineskin,* to be able to hold and accommodate and enjoy **a new relationship with Him.** *To be able to enjoy Him* **for who He truly is.** To be able to enjoy *the new wine of the Spirit,* **the** extravagant love of your Daddy God for YOU!

You see, **the cross does not satisfy the anger of God.** *It satisfies His most holy love.*

The self-sacrifice of Jesus reveals that *God is not the bloodthirsty Deity we imagined.* **It was actually humanity. We** *were the bloodthirsty ones that hated Him and wanted to murder Him.*

And we did murder Him, and many murder Him still today!

God is not the one who has hate and murder in His heart towards us. No, *it's the other way around. God is not the angry Deity we made Him out to be; we were the angry entities,* **the angry ones** *that needed to be satisfied,* **not Him.**

The cross exposes humanity's hostility towards God and rejection of God; it exposes our violence towards Him!

In this act of redemption, in which He allows the evil in us, to do its worst to Him, in this act, in which He demonstrates His love for us, *He totally exposes and thereby destroys all evil (the evil in us and the evil one).*

Colossians 2:14 in the Mirror Bible says,

"...The hands of fallen Man struck the body of Jesus with the blows of their religious hatred and fury when they nailed his bloodied body to the tree; they did not realize that, in the mystery of God's economy, Jesus was the scapegoat of the entire human race!" (Note Isaiah 53:4 & 5)

You see, **the cross was not necessitated** *by an angry, vengeful God who needed appeasement.*

I say again: **The cross was not the necessary payment** *to satisfy a God who is bound by a sense of justice, and therefore demands blood.*

Jesus, who was God incarnate, did not come to save us from God; Jesus did not need to come and save us from His Father, as most evangelicals believe and proclaim.

No, His Father sent Him! *It was Jesus, the Father, and the Holy Spirit, the entire Godhead in co-hoots, working together to redeem us, not with a demand for blood, but with the most amazing display of their love for us, in spite of our demand for their blood.*

In other words, **the wrong idea we had,** in which God is a judge *who just couldn't get over our sin, and demanded blood,* <u>is replaced</u>. It is replaced with *the revelation,* <u>from God</u>, that <u>God is a *Father,*</u> a Daddy, *who simply couldn't get over US, His children.*

It is God, who takes the initiative, *to identify with us, to the uttermost. He stooped down into our hell, and He went to Hell itself and back, to rescue us!* And in doing so, *He brings healing to the victims of evil, who also became the very perpetrators of evil.*

The cross was the entire Godheads' undignified, and yet, most extravagant, public display of affection towards mankind, *just to win our hearts back!*

Jesus reveals a God who would rather face judgment, die, and go to hell Himself, than to live without YOU!

Chapter 5

God's Pursuit Frees From Alternatives!

In 2 Corinthians 5:20 Paul says,

"We implore you, on Christ's behalf, as though God were pleading through us, __be reconciled to God.__"

Paul was writing this to people *who should have had a handle on the truth about God and His love for them, and therefore also about themselves.* But instead **they were losing sight of the truth, *they were growing dull of hearing and hardness of heart was beginning to set in.*** *They were falling back into mere religion, instead of getting caught up in the substance and passion of being in love! ...And all that because of mixed teaching and half-truths.*

*Mixing man-made religious beliefs with what has been revealed in grace, made room for **darkness in their thinking,** about God, and about themselves. This distraction from the truth of their redemption and reconciliation to God, in true friendship and an intimate love-*

relationship, caused them to get caught up again in the flesh, "...**living like mere men;**"

Deception was setting in again. In that state of watered down faith and compromise, *the alternative attractions and addictive narcotic effects of a mere fleshly existence* **was beginning to have a strong appeal and influence upon them again. Sin was beginning to creep in again.**

Living your life by a mere natural-minded identity will lull you to sleep spiritually and trap you in a lesser existence; a lesser experience and expression of life!

Only deception can make *a fake pretense of a life* attractive! The deceptive allurement of this natural world, as well as man-made religious teachings and wrong thinking, *will make you lose track of truth,* and either make you slip back into works and performance in your relationship with God, *or cause you to fall out of love with God, and stop having a personal intimate love-affair with Him.*

Religion is a poor replacement for a genuine relationship with Father God, as Daddy! Religion is rather empty! Even more empty than the lusts (strong, but rather empty desires and passions) of this world!

*Religion instead of **reality;***

*…religion instead of **the reality of God;***

*…religion instead of **reality with God;***

*…without **enjoying God's truth and love;***

*…without an **intimate one-on-one love-affair with Him, which the truth of your origin and redemption affords you;***

…is absolutely empty.

And without that love-affair with God, without that intimate one-on-one relationship with God, wrapped up in His truth, and wrapped up in Him *…**without that reality of God and of love sustaining you, <u>you die inside and begin again to live a hollow shell of a life.</u>** The only other option, the only other alternative, the only other alternative fulfillment then **is to go back to a life of addiction to the flesh,** trying to at least feel alive, **even though you are not!** …Trying to fill the gaping void in your heart **with an inferior love,** the love of self, the love of the world and the flesh and the lusts thereof (strong but rather empty, misguided passions). And in that state of pursuing alternative fulfillment, **you begin to simply neglect and ignore God altogether.***

'Wait a minute brother Rudi. We thought that once we accepted Jesus' sacrifice on our behalf and prayed the sinners' prayer for

salvation that we were reconciled to God, and that we were secure!

Why are you writing this to us?

We have done what our religion requires of us!'

I am sure the people Paul was writing to *may have had the same reaction.* And I can just imagine Paul's response,

'You might think you are totally reconciled in relationship to God, **but reconciliation implies so much more than a distant relationship, so much more than a shallow or fake religious kind of relationship.'**

'Not until you are totally engaged and immersed in intimate friendship and fellowship with God are you actually enjoying what it means to <u>be</u> reconciled with God.'

Relationship *without intimate companionship* is rather empty. **The whole purpose of relationship is *intimate friendship and fellowship.***

In Jeremiah 24:7 God says,

*"I will give them a new heart **to know <u>and to LOVE ME</u>**."*

All He wants is *for us to start embracing His truth and His love,* to stop resisting Him, to stop resisting His truth and His love, and to start resisting Satan and religion, *with its lies and empty deception!*

God didn't *lower His standards of godliness* or somehow *change His design for us* when Jesus came to die for our sins.

He didn't have a compromised standard *of design* in mind for us, <u>*a lesser life*</u> than our authentic original blueprint design.

What is that original blueprint design all about?

It is about living life to the fullest together with Him, giving full expression to that love we enjoy between us and Him, giving full expression to the image and likeness of the One who is love, giving full expression to that authentic life we enjoy, giving full expression to that joy, and that peace, that genuine contentment and that fulfillment and that righteousness, to that love nature and that authentic life together with God we were made to enjoy and give expression to!

Listen, the blood of Jesus doesn't mean that *God has decided to let go of His standards* **and now just conveniently overlooks sin.**

What was previously **unacceptable** *didn't now all of a sudden become* **acceptable** *because* *of the cross.* **God is not into compromise.** If it was *unacceptable* before, **it is still** *unacceptable* **now.**

Sin is unacceptable <u>*because God knows and cannot be fooled by a fake alternative to reality!*</u> *And neither should you!*

<u>*God knows and He has revealed the truth about you.*</u> *He knows and He has revealed* <u>*the truth of your design*</u>*. Everything outside of* <u>*that design*</u> *is a lie and deception. Living any* <u>*inferior kind of life*</u> *to that design is not what He had in mind when He designed you. That alternative is totally unacceptable to Him and should also be to you.*

He wants you to enjoy life together with Him and to *enjoy the life of your original design,* to its fullest, and He knows that *living outside of that design* will only lead to your destruction.

He came to rescue us out of self-destruct mode! Redemption is not God's cop-out, it is God restoring Man <u>*back to his original design, back to an authentic life, back to the way life was meant to be lived*</u>*.*

We weren't designed for sin, but for God and His life, for an *intimate love relationship* with God, giving *full expression* to that *original image and likeness* we were made in.

We were designed to share the life and the glory and the beauty of God!

We were designed to give full expression to the Divine nature; to the love-nature of God!

We were not designed for sin!

God wants us to begin to realize *and believe the love He has for us.* He wants us to begin to realize *and believe what we were designed for.* God wants us *to fall in love with Him as much as He has always been in love with us.*

Have you ever noticed two people that have recently fallen in love? That relationship becomes of utmost importance to them. They are almost never apart. *Their commitment and faithfulness is inspired by their intense love for one another.*

Hey listen, *God wants His initiative to quicken a response of love and devotion from our hearts towards Him.* God won't *share us* with idols, with any fake alternative, and that's a fact.

An idol is anything, any alternative that tries to take His place, even if it is just in subtle ways. It is anything that takes away the allegiance and devotion of your heart to Him.

We must not allow ourselves **to be distracted from that all-fulfilling love-affair with God through wrong, man-made religious ideas or through getting caught up in the love of this world and the things in it!**

We must not allow ourselves to become distracted from the love of God nor from living out our true identity, that image and likeness we were designed to enjoy within ourselves and give expression to!

Jesus, in all His teachings, always brought things back to **the focus of our hearts.** It's all about **the devotion** of our hearts. It's all about **what you _treasure_.**

In Luke 8:14, Jesus talks about *treasuring God's authentic truth and love,* and He talks about **the things that compete** *with God's truth and love and try to prevent God's truth and love from finding its rightful place in our hearts, from germinating, setting down roots, growing and maturing in us, and bearing fruit.*

He put it this way,

"The seed that fell among the thorns and the thistles **represent those who hear the Word of God, but then _choke themselves_ with the worries, riches, and pleasures of this world (they lose their life and joy because they are consumed by the cares of this world, and live their lives for the lusts of the flesh) _and their fruit never matures_.**"

Their relationship with God is never allowed to blossom into a full blown love-affair with Him because His truth and love is not embraced and treasured like it should be. They do not value the truth of God and a love-relationship with God for what it is. They do not value it enough because they do not see much worth in it. Obviously they are deceived and do not even know it!

In Matthew 6:19-33, Jesus encourages us *to embrace and value God's truth and love **above all else.*** He says,

19 *"**Do not lay up for yourselves <u>treasures on earth,</u>** where moth and rust destroy and where thieves break in and steal;*

20 ***but lay up for yourselves treasures in heaven*** *(in the unseen realm of spiritual reality, in spirit dimension, in the realm of spirit truth and relationship with God, in the spirit realm, in your heart, in the realm of true joy and peace and contentment, and life), where neither moth nor rust destroys and where thieves do not break in and steal.*

21 ***For <u>where your treasure is</u>, there your heart will be also.***

22 *The lamp of the body is the eye…"*

In other words, **that which gives you understanding or enlightenment** or that **which influences your way of thinking.** He is talking about **your focus,** about *what you see, what has your attention or devotion, what you really value in life!*

He was really talking about **the influence of** the TRUTH *you focus on,* or **the influence of** the DECEPTION *you choose to focus on.*

"If therefore your eye (your focus; **what has your attention and devotion***) is good;*

…your whole body will be full of light.

23 *"But if your eye (your focus;* **what has your attention and devotion***) is bad* **(if it is inaccurate, or blind, or dark, or negative, or empty, if it has no real substance and fulfillment),** *your whole body will be full of darkness.*

If therefore **the light that is in you** *is darkness,*

…how great is that darkness indeed!"

24 *"***No one can serve (be devoted to) two masters (It's an impossibility);***"*

Your life and your conduct, your whole experience in life, will follow the focus and devotion of your heart!

*"…***for either, you will <u>hate</u> the one and <u>love</u> the other,***"*

Or, let me put it this way:

*"...you will **be loyal (devoted) to the one and despise the other."***

In other words, *it is an unavoidable inevitability*.

"No one can serve (be devoted to) two masters (It's an impossibility);"

"You cannot serve God <u>and</u> mammon (the worship of money, i.e. greed, or a religious devotion to some false god that rules you, some money system, some worldly way of thinking when it comes to money and self-preservation)."

You cannot be <u>devoted to</u> God and be <u>devoted to</u> money and earthly treasures. You will never be able to successfully divide the devotion of your heart like that, it is an impossibility.

The things of the flesh <u>will never be able to compete</u> with the love of God *in value,* or replace it and *become an alternative, a substitute* for it.

You will either be devoted to the one *or the other, <u>but not both</u>!* You are going to have to choose between the two!

He is talking about this internal conflict in our hearts, *this self-destruct mode of pursuing alternative fulfillment, even trying to find it in things that cannot possibly permanently satisfy.* It is a pursuit of sin. In other words, it is missing the point. It is missing the mark. *It is an empty alternative, an empty pursuit outside of our actual design*.

That pursuit of sin *is driven by emptiness.* A conflict of interests within our hearts which cannot be resolved <u>*until*</u> *we grasp the truth of our origin and our redemption and reconciliation back to that origin, back to God our Father, our true Daddy, and the Spirit of truth awakens the love of God in our hearts through revelation into the truth of <u>who we truly are</u> and of <u>our Daddy's love for us</u>.* Only then, through faith, and not before then, *can we actually make the intelligent choice and walk in true friendship with God.*

This love for God and for life and for others, as well as for our true selves, our original design, *is only kindled and kept alive through faith, through an intimate fellowship with God in the TRUTH, sharing His knowledge with Him,* having the same understanding and persuasion of TRUTH and of LOVE and of REALITY as He has!

Developing and maintaining *that persuasion and that intimacy in the TRUTH* takes time to solidify in our hearts, and therefore it demands some undivided attention.

Jesus challenged us again in Matthew 6:25-33 **about being *consumed by the cares of this world* and therefore *living our lives for the lusts of the flesh.*** He said,

25 *"**Do not worry** about your life, what you will eat or what you will drink; nor about your body, what you will put on.*

Is not life more than food and the body more than clothing?"

In other words, ***STOP being driven by anxiety. It becomes a significant distraction to your intimate fellowship with God and your enjoyment of life.***

When we realize and finally believe that God truly, perfectly, loves us, *then we will know that He is trustworthy*. We will KNOW that *He will* take care of us. It will drive *all fear* from our hearts.

26 *"Look at the birds of the air, for **they neither sow nor reap nor gather into barns;***

*...**and YET, your Heavenly Father feeds them.***

Are you not of much more value than they?

27 *Which of you* **by worrying** *can add one cubit (18 inches) to his stature (to his height)?*

28 **So why do you worry** *about your clothing?*

Consider the lilies of the field, **how** *they grow;* **they neither toil nor spin;**

29 **and YET,** *I say to you that even Solomon in all his glory was not arrayed (clothed, or dressed) like one of these.*

30 **Now, if God <u>so</u> clothes the grass of the field, which exists today, and is gone tomorrow,**

...will He not much more clothe you, O you of little faith (of little trust)?

(or of little revelation; of little understanding of the truth – one who is not persuaded by God's truth and love yet)

31 **<u>Therefore</u>, do not worry about your life, saying,**"

'What shall I eat?'

Or, **'What shall I drink?'**

Or, **'What shall I wear?'**

32 **For after all these things the Gentiles <u>seek</u>.**" *(The "gentiles" are the people of this world* **who do not know God and do not**

know the truth of His love and live for the lusts of the flesh.)

*He is talking about **those who hardly have any <u>real</u> relationship with God. They live their lives in the empty pursuit of these things.***

He says,

"<u>Your Heavenly Father knows that you need all these things</u>."

33 *"<u>BUT (as for you,) seek (look for, pursue after, rather desire, treasure, embrace) first</u> the Kingdom of God (His indwelling, His reality, the rule and reign of truth and of His love in your heart) and His righteousness (that spirit identity, that original design and true identity, that image and likeness of Himself which He has placed inside you from the beginning of your existence already),"*

"Seek, pursue after, treasure, embrace and live by these things, enjoy these realities, let them become such a part of who you are, embrace your Daddy's indwelling,"

"...and all these things shall be added to you."

Because, *"<u>Your Heavenly Father knows that you need all these things and shall add them unto you as you need them</u>."*

Jesus re-emphasized these things again in Matthew 10:29-31,

29 *"Are not two sparrows sold for a copper coin?*

And yet, not one of them falls to the ground, apart from your Father's will."

In other words, nothing takes Him by surprise or escapes His attention. He is not unaware of what goes on here on this planet on a split second to split second basis.

That means *God is not some distant, uninterested God living His life in separation from us.* He is not far from any one of us. In Him we live and move and have our being. In Him all things consist, or find their place of belonging and significance and existence

30 *"But the very hairs on your head are all numbered.*

31 **Do not fear <u>THEREFORE</u>;**

<u>You are of more value than many sparrows</u>.*"*

In Matthew 7:13 & 14 we read again how important it is **to become focused and single-minded *when it comes to treasuring God's truth and love in our hearts.***

Jesus used word-pictures and He warns us again,

13 *"Enter by the **narrow gate**," he says;"*

He was talking about being fully persuaded, and therefore single-minded, or narrow-minded, in the truth and love of God.

*"...for **wide** is the gate and **broad is the way that leads to destruction,"***

(Deception can take on many forms.)

*"...**and there are many who go in by it.**"*

Every one of us *has our own believing to do and our own choices to make.* But quite often, people remain messed up in their beliefs and inevitably therefore *make the wrong choices* because, unfortunately then, *they cannot help but continue to have the wrong pursuits.*

How valuable are your pursuits after the things of the flesh really, *in the light of eternity?*

14 *"Because **narrow** is the gate and **difficult (or exclusive, free from distractions) is the way which leads to life,** eternal life, real life, life more abundantly,"*

It is always a challenge to, not only come to the right conclusions in your faith, in what

you believe, but to hold on to those conclusions. It takes genuine revelation into God's truth and love to discover that exclusive, distraction free way of living.

"...and there are few who find it."

Not because it can't be found, *but because many are either too distracted and consumed by the cares of this world, by anxieties and fears, and are therefore too busy living for the lusts of the flesh, or they are too distracted and consumed by this world and the things in this world, too busy living for the lusts of the flesh, the lust of the eyes, and the pride of life!* You see, it is such a subtle thing sometimes!

This is how you can test where your heart is really at: You are still in bondage when you cannot walk away from something. What you cannot walk away from owns you. You will only be truly free from something when you can walk away from it.

It is astonishing how we find an alternative identity and fulfillment in our money and our stuff. Your true fulfillment and identity is not in those things! *The things you own cannot define you or truly add value to your life, neither can your money.* Your worth is not in those things! Life is more than food and clothing! Your value and worth *has been established and forever settled in*

God's heart! It's revealed to you in the price God was prepared to pay *to prove that love, to prove that worth and value to you!*

He loves you!

You are His!

That is your real value and worth!

You belong in your Daddy's heart!

That is where you belong!

That is the only place where your heart can find *its true acceptance and fulfillment, its place of true belonging, value, and worth!*

Sure, God wants us to be blessed and to have things, *but it is astounding how easily our souls get attached to and looks for alternative satisfaction from our money and our things, because we lose sight of who we truly are and where our true satisfaction, value, and worth actually lie.*

Instead of owning things, *the things end up owning us,* and in the *empty pursuit* of obtaining those things *we lose sight of everything else of true value, we even lose ourselves!*

In Proverbs 23:4 & 5, we find an instruction, which is more than just good advice.

4 *"Do not overwork to be rich;*

*…**because of what you already know,** I beg of you, **cease!***

5 *Will you set your eyes on that **which is not?** (...which is worth very little, and doesn't last?)*

For riches certainly make themselves wings, they fly away *like an eagle toward heaven."*

Paul also instructed his spiritual son, Timothy, and warned him, and us, in 1 Timothy 6:6-11,

6 *"Godliness **with <u>contentment</u> is great gain."***

Being content with being your Daddy's child, *living life with Him and acting like Him* **is great gain [*true riches*]. It is the only thing that adds true and lasting value and fulfillment to your life.**

7 *"For we brought nothing into this world; **and it is certain, we can carry nothing out.***

8 *And having food and clothing, **with these we shall be <u>content</u>.***

9 **But those who desire to be rich (those who pursue empty alternatives, worldly riches and fake temporary treasures);**

*…**they fall into temptation and a snare;***

...and into many foolish and harmful lusts (strong but rather empty desires and addictions);

These many foolish and harmful lusts (these strong but rather empty desires, passions and alternative pursuits) *drown men in destruction and perdition.*

10 *For **THE LOVE** of money and things, is a root of all kinds of evil;*

...some have strayed from the true Christian faith in their greediness;

...and pierced themselves through with many sorrows.

11 *But you, O man and woman of God, **flee these things** and pursue righteousness!"*

Pursue your true identity and your original design instead. Pursue intimate friendship and fellowship with God instead. Pursue a life free from the lusts of the flesh, free from empty, temporary alternative fulfillment that is not true fulfillment at all. No matter how strong the appeal of those temptations and illusions and deceptions are, they remain an empty pursuit of alternative fulfillment outside of God's love and friendship. By now you should know it's a lie, a mirage; a ruse. *"...pursue godliness, faith, love, patience and gentleness (instead)."*

James, the natural born brother of Jesus Himself, also warned us in James 3:16,

*"Where **self-seeking** and envy exist;*

(These things are the fruit of deception, the fruit of the Fall. Where these things continue to exist), **confusion and every other evil thing will be there also.***"

He says also in James 4:1-5,

1 *"Why do you fight with everything and everybody?"*

In other words, *where does most of the stress, raging within you, and within your life come from?*

"Does it not come from your <u>desires</u> for pleasure, warring within you?"

Does it not come from the <u>lusts</u>, *from the strong but rather empty desires of the flesh,* of the natural-minded and natural-oriented Man?

2 *"You desire (you passionately lust after) and do not have and so you are angry with others and use and abuse your relationships, because you covet and cannot obtain* (and when you do, *it doesn't fulfill you.*)

You fight and war all the time...

3 *You pray and ask **and do not receive,** because you ask amiss, **that you may spend it on your pleasures.***

4 **Adulterers and adulteresses!**

Do you not know that friendship with this world is enmity (It causes serious conflict in your heart when it comes to your devotion in a love-relationship) with God?*"*

It distorts truth and robs you of everything God has in mind for you in relationship with Him and others.

Outside of God's love, outside of that love also reigning and finding expression in us, what do we really truly have?

*"***Whoever therefore wants to be a friend of this world <u>makes himself</u> God's enemy once again***."*

It is not God who becomes your enemy, *it is you who drift away and end up resisting and opposing everything good God desires for you and for others.*

You end up living as if Jesus never even came and revealed the truth and the love of God for you, and redeemed your life!

5 *"Or does the Scripture say in vain, 'The Spirit who dwells in us **yearns jealously!**'"*

Listen, God yearns after you! His desire is for you! He wants intimate friendship, fellowship, companionship, and devotion …a soul mate!

It is only the knowledge of the truth, and the love of our Daddy God that can truly set us free **and cause us to finally embrace the fact,** <u>*the reality,*</u> **that** *we have been delivered from the power of darkness.*

If we correctly understand God's love for us we will know that we cannot abuse it. *And if we begin to enjoy and treasure that intimate love-relationship with Him, as much as He does with us,* **we will not tolerate the empty pursuit of alternatives in our lives.** We will begin to hate sin and idolatry as much as He does.

You cannot say, *'I love Him, BUT I love this sin too.'* **That's being deceived, that's becoming familiar, and that's playing games with God.** *Jesus didn't die so you can continue in sin: an empty pursuit of alternatives, an empty pursuit of that which is fake and not real!*

Jesus didn't die so you could continue in an empty pursuit of alternative fulfillment that does not even satisfy!

Paul warns us against entertaining sin in our lives in Romans 6:1 & 2,

1 *"Shall we now continue in sin that grace may just continue to abound?*

2 *Certainly not!"*

Living with that kind of casual attitude towards sin and towards God's love, living with that kind of double-mindedness about your love-relationship with God is detestable and disgusting, an abomination to God, and rightly so! The Scriptures calls it *becoming lukewarm.*

Have you ever enjoyed a lovely glass of lukewarm water?

…no?

…my point exactly!

In Revelation 3:15-20, we read about some Christians **who developed wrong attitudes *because they deceived themselves,*** *and therefore it turned their Christianity into an unpalatable, vomitus thing, even to God, and I am sure to others also.*

He said to them,

15 *"I know your works, that you are neither cold nor hot. I could wish you were cold or hot.*

16 ***So then, because you are lukewarm, and neither cold nor hot, I will spew you out of My mouth.****"*

They may have thought, *'What are you talking about Lord?'* And I can just imagine His response to them, *Listen, the reason why I feel this way about you is,*

17 *"...**because you say, 'I am rich, have become wealthy, and have <u>need</u> of nothing'***

*...**<u>and yet</u> you do not know that you are wretched, miserable, poor, blind, and naked.***"

He goes on to say in Verse 18,

18 *"I counsel you to buy from Me gold, refined in the fire,"*

He is talking about *faith* that is pure, *a heart full of pure devotion to God!* **Its passion is derived directly from God's Truth and love.**

That kind of *faith and love* **is more precious than even fine gold.**

He essentially says,

*'Let My faith in you and about you **inspire your faith and love and become the source of your faith and love'***

*"...that you may be **truly rich;***

...and (receive from Me) **white garments** (**undefiled,** like a bride's white dress on her wedding day);

…so that you may be **clothed** (with a heart full of love and faith and pure devotion,);

…so that the shame of your nakedness may not be revealed;

…and anoint your eyes with eye salve, **so that you may see***! (...***so that you may no longer be deceived, so that you may no longer be blinded by deception, by self-delusion and hypocrisy, by that which is fake, by alternative false fulfillment; so that you may see** what I see, **so that you may** see the truth, **so that you may** see My love for you***).*

19 **As many as I love, I rebuke and chasten (through confronting them with the truth).**

Therefore be zealous (be eager) and repent.*"*

"Repent" *or* **"METANOIA"** in the Greek, means – **to come to such a revelation of the truth, that it may radically change your mind, your way of thinking about yourself and about life and about God and about others to such a degree that it changes your heart attitude and your actions towards yourself and towards God and towards others.**

God says,

20 *"Behold I stand at the door and knock. If anyone hears My voice and opens the door, I*

will come in to him, and dine with him, and he with Me."

He is talking about our enjoyment of one another, Him and us united, on the same page in true friendship. He is talking about having sweet, intimate "KOINONIA" or "fellowship" together in genuine, pure love for each other.

If you are one of those Christians who are dabbling in (and secretly in love with) pornography, *you are ruled by lust my friend.* You are ruled by a strong *but rather empty* desire. **It is the oldest, *most inner destructive addiction known to man,* and it has become your pet sin, your empty idol you cling to and protect *through self-delusion and self-deception.* But you, too, can be free today!**

Don't be like so many who, when they find out *God does not approve of their destructive pattern,* respond,

'Well, I'm only human.' or, 'I'm only looking, what's the harm in that?'

'I'm not hurting anybody!'

They often say to me,

'It's okay. I don't care what you say. God still loves me. Besides, I am only appreciating His creation.'

But no, listen; actually, quite the opposite is true. **They are *degrading* God's creation; not appreciating it. It is not art. It is sin! They are in self-destruct mode *and they are unknowingly dragging others into it.* They have disrespected God's creation, His masterpiece, the human body! *Not only their own, but that of other people as well.***

According to Jesus, ***they have already*** *committed fornication or adultery* in their heart. **They have stripped the human body of dignity and *degraded* a holy thing *into something of very little value. We are all of much more value than that!***

Paul asks some very pertinent questions of some Christians in 1 Corinthians 6. And in asking those questions, he explains things that should be obvious, *at least to everyone who calls themselves a lover of God or a believer and a Christian.*

He says in verse 15 and also in verse 18-20,

15 *"**Do you not know that your bodies are members of Christ?***

Shall I then take the members of Christ and make them members of a harlot; or engage those members even in homosexuality?

...Certainly not!"

Obviously, he is not talking about marriage between one man and one woman here, which is wholesome and a natural institution by God. That marriage between one man and one woman, and the intimacy they enjoy with each other, is pure and born out of love, and it is a prophetic picture pointing to the spiritual intimacy and union we enjoy between us and God.

Such a thing as marriage and intimacy with another person within that marriage is not something we enter into casually in the natural. It is not something that is available and open to outsiders. *And in the spiritual it is exactly the same.*

This love relationship we enjoy with our Maker is not to be entered into in casual devotion! It is such a sacred thing in both the natural and the spiritual and it has spiritual consequences when we begin to fall into idolatry in this area of our lives and look to that idol for false alternative fulfillment.

That is why Paul, by inspiration of the Holy Spirit of God, says in Verse 18,

18 *"Flee sexual immorality.*

*Every sin that a man does is outside the body ...but he who commits sexual immorality **sins against his own body (and the body of the person he is committing the fornication with)."***

He continues in verse 19,

19 *"Or do you not know that your body is the temple of the Holy Spirit, who is in you,*

...whom you have from God;

...and you are not your own?

20 **For you were bought at the highest price;**

...therefore glorify God in your body and in your spirit;

...which are God's!"

He says and reiterates again in 1 Corinthians 10:21 & 22,

21 *"You cannot drink the cup of the Lord and the cup of demons;*

...you cannot partake of the Lords table and the table of demons.

22 **Or do we provoke the Lord to jealousy?**

Are we stronger than Him?"

He says in Hebrews 12:14,

"Pursue (that) holiness (the holiness of love and pure devotion to God that truth and faith alone awaken), without which no one

will <u>see</u> (will be able to have a genuine relationship and friendship with) the Lord."

Paul tries his best in Hebrews 2:3 to exhort us,

"Don't neglect so great a salvation."

In Galatians 5:1 he says,

"<u>Stand fast therefore;</u>

...<u>in the liberty by which Christ has made us free;</u>

...and do not be entangled again with a yoke of bondage."

Chapter 6

Abiding in the Son and in the Father

John made these profound statements in 1 John 5:18-21,

18 *"We know that whoever is born of God does not (continue in) sin, but he who has been born of God <u>keeps himself</u> (that means you can), and the wicked one does not touch him.*

19 *We know that we are of God* (even though) *the whole world lies under the <u>sway</u> (influence, manipulation of) the wicked one."*

It's the knowledge **that we are of God; that His image and likeness is our true identity,** *it is that knowledge that you are His offspring and that He truly loves you <u>that becomes the fuel for change in your behavior</u>.*

God has revealed truth. He has made available to you *His reality.*

Why continue in a *lesser* reality?

Why live a lesser life when *authentic life* **stares you right in the face?**

I mean, in the light of *the real truth about you* **revealed** by God Himself, *why live a lie? Why continue in an empty, fake existence!*

20 *"And we know that* **the Son of God has come and <u>has given us understanding</u>;**

...**so that we may know Him who is true;**

...<u>*and we are in Him who is true;*</u>

...*in His Son, Jesus Christ.*

This is the true God, and eternal life.

21 **Little children, <u>keep yourselves from idols</u>!"**

God has laid aside all the hurt and disappointment of the past *and revealed the truth.*

Now, *"repentance"*, or *METANOIA* (a radical and complete change of mind about us and about God and about others; a total change of heart attitude and actions towards ourselves and towards Him and towards others), *is the only appropriate response.*

Paul then also says in 2 Corinthians 7:1,

1 *"Therefore, having these exceedingly great and precious promises, or realities, beloved,* **let us cleanse ourselves from all filthiness of the flesh and spirit!**

...<u>perfecting holiness</u> (perfecting our enjoyment of righteousness; our intimate relationship with God in the truth, as well as our expression of our righteousness, of our original design and true, authentic spirit identity) <u>in the fear (in the respect, love, and adoration) of God</u>.*"*

In 1 John 3:3, John also says,

"And everyone who has **this hope** *in Him..."*

(Everyone who has **this living desire and expectation** *of enjoying God's friendship and closeness, and of enjoying righteousness, and an eternal life with God;*

Everyone who has a desire for these things and has an expectation of enjoying these things,) **purifies himself, just as He is pure.***"*

In verse 7 he says that,

7 *"**He who practices righteousness**...*

(He who practices the truth as it is revealed by God; He who practices intimate relationship with God and walks in true fellowship and friendship with God *by believing and embracing these things* *concerning salvation and the redemption of their original design and true identity,)*

...is righteous, just as He is righteous."

That is why Paul says in Romans 8:1,

1 *"There is, therefore, NOW no condemnation for those who are in Christ Jesus;*

(For those who abide in the reality of their union with Him)

...who walk according to the Spirit (according to their true spirit identity and design) and do not walk according to the flesh (according to their natural identity, according to that old, fallen, deceived mindset inherited from the Fall)."

Hallelujah!!!

John says in 1 John 2:1,

1 *"...these things I write to you so that you may not sin."*

In other words: Wake up! Snap out of it! Grow up! The grace of God is not an excuse for sin!

And then he says, *"IF anyone sins* (not **when,** but **IF** anyone does blow it and gets lured into a temptation)..."

John says, *"...we have an advocate with the Father, Jesus Christ the righteous."*

And this is also not a license to sin or giving you an excuse or making room for weakness. Jesus is not up in Heaven right now *defending our wrong actions* before the Father. He is not up there *trying to work a little deal with God* on our behalf, saying something like,

'Hey, Father, let's just give so-and-so another chance, okay? Look how they're struggling down there ...at least so-and-so is trying.'

No! Jesus' advocacy is a legal office. Its reality is founded in His blood, in His substitutionary work on the cross, *by which we were forgiven and redeemed.*

His advocacy is for *our* benefit. **If He is arguing any case right now, *it is not before God,* it's before *you*. He is trying to get you to see *the Truth and to believe and embrace and abide in it.***

You see, God is not fooling Himself. He clearly sees and knows everything, *but He prefers to live by a greater Truth about you.* He fills His mind, *not with your sin,* but with the reality *of the New Covenant,* the reality *of you being His child, of you being a New Creation.* And *He wants you to do the same.*

He wants these truths to so fill your heart and mind that *they become greater;* that they become *of greater reality* ...*that they become of greater consequence, and influence than what the natural has to say about you.* He wants these truths to completely fill your heart and mind.

Why?

Because it is the only way for you to consistently walk free and stay free.

If you find yourself in the mud, *get up and get out of that mess!*

Quit struggling with your struggling and *get caught up in God's love and God's eternal truth about you!*

In 1 John 2:6 John says,

6 *"He who says he **abides** in Him;*

*...**ought himself (naturally, as a result of that abiding in Him);***

*...**also then, to walk just as He walked**."*

This is not wishful thinking.

The ability to do this, the ability to walk *abiding in Him,* to walk *abiding in the truth,* to walk *just as He walked,* is a reality *to those who set their heart* (not just their mind, *but their heart*) on *believing and embracing The Truth, and* therefore practicing *The Truth;* practicing *righteousness.*

These things are a reality to the genuine believer, not the hypocrites, but to the real Christian. Or else John, and God through John's writings, never would have said so.

How do we get there?

John gives us the answer plainly in 1 John 2:24,

24 *"Therefore, let that* **abide** *in you* **which you heard** *(concerning that which was) from the beginning.*

If **what you heard** *(concerning that which was) from the beginning* **abides** *in you,* **you also will abide in the Son and in the Father."**

Again, this *abiding,* **this** *dwelling,* **is not a casual thing.**

Paul said in his second letter to the Corinthians, in Chapter 11, Verse 2,

"I betrothed you to Christ, **to be a chaste virgin.***"*

How in the world did Paul accomplish this? What did He use *to impact their hearts to such a degree* that they would **actually do it?**

The answer is found in Ephesians 5:25-27.

He did it, *"By the washing of the water of the Word of His love (the Word, the gospel about God's love, the message about Jesus' love)."*

That gospel, that Word about Father God's love and about Jesus' love had the same purifying effect upon their hearts as a thorough washing would have upon the body.

So, in the light of what we have heard, in the light of such tremendous love as God has for us, in the light of being totally reconciled and restored to intimate relationship with God, our true Daddy, in the light of such tremendous truth revealed and made known to us concerning our original design and true, authentic spirit identity *revealed and restored to us in Jesus, in that great work of redemption, let us no longer* **disappoint ourselves.**

Disappoint ourselves?

Instead of fulfilling us, *our idols, our false alternative pursuits of fulfillment leave us empty.* We think they bring us happiness, *but that fountain of happiness dries up very quickly.* Then it's on to the next thing and the next thing again, *BUT the void remains.*

Our true fulfillment is only found in intimate companionship, friendship, and fellowship with God. It is only found in being our Father's image and likeness, expressing that Divine nature; that love nature!

True fulfillment is only found in living out our true, authentic spirit identity and original authentic design, *our true design as children of God*. It is only found in intimate companionship, friendship, and fellowship with God, our Father, *our Daddy, in living life together with Him*.

So, let us not disappoint God either!

Disappoint God?

Yes, Paul greets the saints in Ephesians 6:23 & 24, and this is what he says,

23 *"Peace to the brethren, and **love with faith**, from God the Father and the Lord Jesus Christ.*

24 *Grace (God's favor and friendship) be **with all those who love our Lord Jesus Christ in sincerity**."*

He says, *"...love with faith from God the Father and the Lord Jesus Christ..."*

God put it all on the line. He gave His heart to us on a platter. He *entrusted us* with His love. He trusts us with His heart, with His

satisfaction and fulfillment, with His deepest emotions, with His friendship.

Listen, Satan wants us to continue to focus on religious do's and don'ts. He wants you *to keep your eyes* **on yourself and your conduct. He always plays on your emotions and feelings of guilt and regret.**

That is what sin-consciousness is all about! It's about **focusing on what I did wrong, or what I should have done, or should be doing.**

Focusing on that, will give you an inferiority complex, and what is even worse, **God's desire for intimate friendship and fellowship with <u>you</u> will remain unmet.**

If Satan can play on your emotions and get you to be sin-conscious all the time, **you will automatically draw away, every time you want to** *draw near* **to God.**

God was stating the obvious when He said,

"If anyone draws back, My soul **has no pleasure** *in him."* (Hebrews 10:38)

How can you draw pleasure from a relationship *if the person who is the object of your desire* <u>constantly cowers in your presence</u>?

It reminds me of when I was in High School and still suffered from a terrible inferiority complex. Every time the most beautiful girl among the cheerleaders (correction: she was the most beautiful girl in school) would talk to me, I would clam up and get all goofy. I would cower in her presence with nothing to say. Words would elude me.

All I could think was, *'What would she want with a loser like me?'*

My friends and her friends would tell me all the time that she liked me, *but I didn't believe them.* Somehow *it was just too much for me to grasp* that a girl, as beautiful as her, would want anything to do with me. *We never did develop a relationship.*

Thank God for salvation and *"METANOIA!"* Thank God for my beautiful wife Carmen. He truly did redeem my life and save me from that inferiority complex.

Ephesians 2:4 and 1:6 tells us exactly how God our Father, our Daddy, feels about us, what value we have to Him, and what He did in order to have an intimate relationship with us!

"But God, who is <u>rich</u> in mercy;

...because of His <u>great love</u> with which He loves us..."

Ephesians 1:6 says,

"By <u>His grace</u> He has made us accepted in the Beloved (in Jesus)."

God wants us to begin to grasp what Paul wrote about in Ephesians 3:18 & 19.

He wants us to grasp,

"…the length and the breadth, the height and the depth of His love, <u>which surpasses understanding</u>…"

This thing is *a heart thing,* not just a head thing! You see, your head can get tired of hearing, 1 + 1 = 2. You can easily get bored with it, but your heart can never get tired of hearing, *"I love you."* Especially if it comes from someone close to us, who really means what they say!

Paul prayed for us to get a revelation of these things. He prayed for us in Romans 15:13 that,

*"**God may <u>FILL US with all joy and peace;</u>**

…IN BELIEVING."

John also said in 1 John 4:16,

*"We know **and have believed** <u>the love God has for us</u>."*

He says in verse 19 (1 John 4:19),

*"We love Him **because He first loved us**."*

You see, *this thing **is a heart thing,** not just a head thing!*

He says, in 1 John 1:2,

"The life was manifested;

...**and we** *have seen, and bear witness, and* **declare to you;**

...**that eternal life;**

...**which was with the Father;**

...**and was manifested to us."**

Can you see that it is **a faith thing, *an embrace from the heart?***

It's not just a knowledge thing, not just a head thing, not just a mind thing, **but *a heart thing!***

John says in 1 John 1:1-4,

1 *"That which was from the beginning, which we have heard, (not just with our natural ears, but with our spiritual ears, with the heart);*

...*which we have seen, (not just with our natural eyes, but with our spiritual eyes, with the heart);*

...*which we have looked upon, (gazed upon, beheld, focused our attention upon);*

...and which our hands have also handled, (which we have also experienced);

*...**concerning the Word of life...**"*

He says,

'...these things, these truths, this love message...'

3 *"**we declare (we make it known) <u>to you</u>, so that you also may have <u>this fellowship</u> with us, and <u>truly</u> <u>our</u> <u>fellowship</u> <u>is</u> with the Father and with His Son Jesus Christ.***

4 ***These things we write to you, so that <u>your joy may be full</u>!*"**

Chapter 7

The Love We Have for One Another

Now, in the light of all that has been said, Paul says this to us in Philippians 2:5-9,

5 *"Let this mind <u>be in you</u> which was also in Christ Jesus,*

6 *who, being in the form of God, did not consider it robbery to be equal with God."*

In other words, Jesus enjoying equality with God did not take away from who God is! The Son, wanting that equality, wanting to be associated with His Father, wanting to be seen as being equal to God, did not rob God of anything! No father gets offended when his children act like him and try to put on His shoes and walk in his shoes.

The Father likes it when we are imitators of Him and when we want an intimate relationship of equality with Him. He likes it when we want friendship, companionship, and face to face encounters of intimacy with Him. He even likes it when we want to learn how to walk in, and begin to practice

His authority with Him, destroying the works of the evil one, in laying hands on the sick, and doing miracles, and rescuing people out of darkness and ignorance, by sharing the light of the gospel with them.

So, Christ Jesus,

6 *"who, being in the form of God, did not consider it robbery to be equal with God."*

He did not consider equality, His Divine attributes or external characteristics and station as God, **as something to be held onto** – meaning His Omnipotence, Omniscience, etc.

7 *"but made Himself **of no reputation**…"*

That means He emptied Himself of His privileges.

*"…**taking the form of a servant,** and coming in the likeness of Man."*

8 *"And being found in appearance as a man, **He humbled Himself;***

*…**and became obedient to the point of death,** even the death of the cross.*

9 ***Therefore, God also has highly exalted Him*** *and given Him the name which is above every name…"*

This scripture describes the incarnation in which the Son laid aside His privileges as God. He laid aside His Divine attributes of Omnipotence, Omniscience and all the rest, *and yet He retained the core of His person. He remained, in very essence, the God who is **love**, even though He took on flesh and became a man.*

He became a man, Jesus of Nazareth, and as a man, he became our example, *not an example for us, **but an example of us**. He lived his life as a man, and yet still a partaker of the divine nature, **just as we are.***

*As a man he lived his life as the exact representation of the invisible God; the manifest expression of the image and likeness of God our Father; the God who is **love!***

Jesus as a man, lived his life in fellowship with the Father, he lived his life sensitive to the Holy Spirit's voice and leading within him, and so the very power and majesty, He, God the Son, laid aside in becoming a man, he as a man still had access to in fellowship with God the Father, in the spirit.

He lived his life conscious of his true identity as son of God, and of the indwelling Spirit of God, *thus he manifested the love of God, as well as the power of God, as he walked in fellowship with God.*

You see; in this incarnation, in this act of becoming Man, **God humbled Himself and became a servant to Mankind!**

Yet, *because He remained the God who is love and did it as an act of love,* **He was not reduced in person or dignity.**

We can see this same thing play out in John 13 where Jesus *put on a towel or apron **and washed His disciples' feet.*** He, being their teacher, being looked up to and respected as Master, *was totally free. He was totally free to humble Himself in this act of service <u>without losing His dignity or value</u>.*

In a sense, we can see how the incarnation and ascension *are totally related and linked to one another.* **God humbled Himself and the Son of God became the Son of Man, so that the sons of Man might again be restored to be the sons of God.**

The ascension is the glorification of both Jesus *and Man. Man was glorified in* **Christ!**

God honored Jesus, and in so doing, *also honored and restored us* **to that place and position of glory (which He intended for us** *from the beginning.) We were elevated again to a place of <u>union and equality with God in relationship</u>.*

Just as God became Man *without ceasing to be God,* just so, *we have been inseparably united with God without ceasing to be human beings.*

Union and equality of being with God in spirit and relationship *does not consume us. But rather, it* releases us *to be* truly *ourselves.*

We remain *distinct* human beings, people, *even though we are in union with God,* but we become *what Man was always meant to be.*

We become people full of love, and full of God's Spirit and power, the exact image and likeness of the invisible God on display, just like Jesus was in His earthly existence!

My point is this: **When you are fulfilled in the love of God, when you are** secure *in the knowledge of who you are,* **in the knowledge of** *your true identity;* **when you are** secure *in who you are,* **when you are** secure **in your true identity and the love of your Daddy God, when you are** secure **in your sonship,** *then pride is not an issue for you anymore.*

Humbling yourself in service to others is not beneath you, *but it becomes your joy* **because such deeds of love and service actually confirm the unchanging character**

of your true identity. It actually confirms the truth of who you really are.

You are spirit, and you are LOVE. We are love children of a love God.

WE ARE SPIRIT, AND WE ARE LOVE! And we have authority over darkness!

You see, **God demonstrated to us, *and then Jesus gave to us, a new mode of living!* He came to teach us what the image and likeness of our Daddy, *the God who is love,* is all about!**

He came and He taught us *to love one another!*

He taught us to love everyone as brothers and sisters, all people, no matter what race they are, or background they come from, and especially so if they are fellow Christians, whether they believe the same way we do or not.

He said in John 15:12,

"This is My commandment, that you love one another, just as I have loved you. This I command you, that you love one another."

Why give us a command? Why do the Scriptures use the word, *"command?"*

Because He strongly wants to persuade us that authentic life can only be found and lived in Love, in God, in fellowship with the Spirit of God!

You weren't meant to live life on your own terms! Living a self-centered, selfish, loveless life *is a life lived in self-destruct mode.*

We were designed to live life *in the context of family.* God, our Father, our Daddy, is building His *family.* The body of Christ, the *"Church", is all about family;* it is *all about intimate connection and friendship with God, and with one another* - Ephesians 2:19.

True Christianity is *all about relationship, it's all about* genuine connection and interaction with God and with one another.

We weren't designed to live life in isolation.

Love and life only thrives in the context of true relationship, in the context of true friendship and family. *Authentic life can only be lived in harmony with others.*

Love is so much more than a feeling! It's *so much more than cozy, warm feelings and thoughts towards others.* Love is so much more than *mere good intentions!*

That is why Jesus, in another place, made it clear that *He wants us to reconcile and make*

amends with everyone, <u>even our enemies</u>, as much as it is up to us, *as much as it is possible.*

He said, *"<u>**Love**</u> **your enemies;"***

That means people that you used to hate for any reason, or that may still hate you, for whatever reason.

*"Bless those who curse you, **do good to those who hate you, and** (genuinely) **pray** (with a heart full of love) **for those who** (abuse their relationship with you and) **spitefully use you"***
- Matthew 5:43-48

Not because you are becoming someone's doormat, not because you have an inferiority complex or can't see when you're being despised or being manipulated for someone else's self-serving reasons, ***but because that life of love is the only life you can now live.***

A life of genuine love is the only authentic life; it is a life of restoration of relationships, and creating new ones; lasting friendships.

Of course, I am not saying to put yourself deliberately in those negative situations. If you can avoid a negative, detrimental situation and get out of such an abusive environment, then by all means, *do so.*

And don't do something stupid. Don't be dumb, man, use your brain *when it comes to loving your enemies.* If you show up at your enemy's door, *you might get his fist* rather than his hand of friendship. *But at the opportune time, **if you keep praying in love and wait for the right time,** like, say, **when your enemy needs help or finds himself in trouble, if you show up then to bless him and love him and help him in a practical way,** he might just change his heart towards you!*

*Softening a bitter or hard heart, **as well as cultivating a genuine friendship** always takes sincerity and commitment **and requires genuine love and giving of yourself even when it is inconvenient.***

How do you actually prefer and befriend another person?

You change your schedule *and go out of your way, in love, for that person.*

That's how you make a friend:

…by meeting a need;

…or by being a friend!

*Quite often it may cost you something, **but nothing genuine and of true value comes cheap!*** **God came to win our friendship and restore our relationship with Him, *at great personal cost to Himself!*** **God genuinely** loved the world so exceedingly much, *that He gave!* Generosity and giving of oneself *is the hallmark of love and friendship!*

I say again:

The only authentic life *is a life of harmony and unity and friendship with others, a life of generosity and giving of oneself!* **If you ask God, He will lead you and help you get connected with other genuine Christian believers,** *to befriend and fellowship with.*

Ask Him to connect you with true Christians that have a handle on this revelation of their true identity revealed and restored in Jesus Christ in His successful work of redemption. They will share with you and help you understand and live these things more fully and thoroughly. *They will love you and be there for you as family, because after all,* **we are**!

You may be my brother from another mother, BUT WE ALL HAVE THE SAME FATHER... ha... ha... ha...

I cannot emphasize enough how crucial it is for you to develop real relationships, genuine friendships, *and become a part of the extended family of God.*

Satan is always trying to cause division *through the breakdown of relationships.*

If he can get you **isolated,** he can stunt your progress in the full appropriation of truth and love in your life, *and keep you from advancing in the love of God, in every good thing that is in you, in Christ Jesus. Many of those qualities cannot be developed or appropriated in isolation.*

If the devil can get you **isolated,** *he can then also keep you from making an impact by promoting the love of God and every good thing in other people's lives as well.*

Paul said in Philemon 1:6 that,

"I pray that your participation (or your mutual sharing) in the faith (in other words, your friendship and fellowship with other believers) will become effectual (it will only become effective, impacting and meaningful) in the mutual acknowledging of every good thing that is already within us in our union with Christ Jesus."

We need friendship and fellowship with other believers.

Paul says in another place that since we are the body of Christ together, and individually, and therefore members of one another, the hand cannot say to the foot, *'I have no need of you!'* Or, how can the eye say to the hand, *'I can do without you!'*

To say that, *'I want to be a Christian, but I don't want to belong to a local church fellowship or body of believers,'* is not the language of love, it's not the language of Christ, it would be the same as saying, *'I want to be married and stay single!'* What you are saying makes no sense!

Listen, we were all immersed by one Spirit into love; therefore we were all immersed by one Spirit into one body, *in Christ Jesus, in His work of redemption. And when we entered into faith,* there is only one faith, one Lord, *and one immersion into one body, because of love!* We are all members of that body, individually, and corporately, together, because we are all the members of Christ, individually and together as a whole.

When you became a believer, therefore, whether you realize it or not, you entered into the family of God. And in all reality you became a member of His household, the household of faith (Galatians 6:10). You became part of *the bride of Christ;* you became a member of the body of Christ, an expression of His love, an expression of His *"Church;"* **His body of believers.** Whether you like it or not, you are a vital part of the *"Church",* corporately *and locally.* That implies belonging to a group of people as friends and true family who love each other, *rather than to an institution.*

Just as Jesus surrounded Himself with the twelve disciples and the many other followers and friends He associated with as friends and family in His day, we need to be with other followers and friends of Jesus.

The Scriptures, and the Holy Spirit who inspired those Scriptures, teaches us that the Christian faith is a *'together'* faith. When you become a genuine Christian, the Holy Spirit not only brings you into relationship and friendship with God as Father, as your Daddy, *but He also brings you into relationship and friendship with other people too.*

When you became a believer, you became a part of God's people, the *"Church,"* living on earth everywhere, even locally, right in your back yard, in your area, in the area where you live.

Just make sure that the people you connect to and make friends with and fellowship with *are genuine believers **who genuinely believe and understand the real gospel,*** and are not just religious people who aren't *even filled with the Holy Spirit,* involved with some man-made, religious Christianity!

There are some very sincere people out there, *and there are some real fakes out there too.* But there are plenty of sincere ones, and sincerely ignorant too. **So beware,** not everything that carries the Christian label is real Christianity!

Don't let this scare you off though.

Remember this: **Two is better than one, and a three-fold cord is not easily broken.**

Ask Father God to help you.

Venture out and allow Him to lead you in finding genuine believers who know and live the truths I am writing about in this book, whom you can befriend and fellowship with.

Jesus said that the world would come to know Him *by the love we have for one another.* It is His desire for us to walk in the unity of truth, not some fake, pretend unity based on compromise. He desires for us to walk in the truth of redemption and the kind of love and family it promotes, *and together make a difference* in this world we live in.

I say again: **as far as it is up to you, walk in love and forgiveness towards <u>everyone</u>.**

In 1 Peter 4:8, Peter instructs us,

*"And **<u>above all things</u>** have fervent love for one another, for 'Love will cover a multitude of sins.'"*

Paul also talks about this Christian family dynamics in Ephesians 4:32,

*"And be kind to one another, tenderhearted, **forgiving one another, just as God in Christ also forgave you.**"*

In Colossians 3:12 & 13 he says,

12 *"Therefore, as God's own chosen people, holy and beloved, put on tender mercies, kindness, humbleness of mind, meekness, long suffering;*

13 *bearing with one another (putting up with one another's idiosyncrasies or personality differences);*

…and forgiving one another, if anyone has a complaint against another;

…even as Christ forgave you, <u>so you also must do</u>."

In these Scriptures and in these instructions, *Paul was revealing the Father's design for us because that is what He is like! He is love and love forgives!* We are made in His image and likeness. Therefore we are love, and love forgives! PERIOD! No ifs, ands, or buts!

Now, having said all that, I also do want to add the following conclusion in the Gospel:

We must appreciate that the love of God is filled with forgiveness, and it is unfailing, *but it is also not a weak, wishy-washy, compromising thing!*

To love and accept a person *does not mean we are to entirely overlook and now*

condone their sin. That is not the love of God. That is an inferior representation of the love of God.

We are to love people absolutely and without compromise, wanting to see them totally free from the sin that is destroying their lives; wanting to see them totally free from living life in self-destruct mode. Otherwise, it isn't genuine love! It isn't the genuine love of God! It isn't Christian love!

<u>Authentic love</u> always reveals the truth of redemption and of the love of God and of our freedom to give expression to our original design and true identity, and so rescues loved-ones out of sin, out of a pursuit of empty alternative fulfillment; living life in self-destruct mode!

James encourages us with these words in James 5:19 & 20,

19 *"Brethren, if anyone among you <u>wanders from The Truth</u>, **and someone turns him back,***

20 *let him know that he who turns a sinner <u>from the error of his way</u> **will save a soul out of death and destruction,** and so 'cover a multitude of sins.'"*

Paul essentially says the same thing in Galatians 6:1 & 2,

1 *"Brethren, if a man is overtaken in any trespass, you who are spiritual **restore (rescue)** such a one **in a spirit of gentleness** (not in a spirit of condemnation and judgment), considering yourself, lest you also be tempted (tempted to be self-righteous and prideful and judgmental and to also therefore not act like your true self as a child of God and partaker of the Divine nature; of the love-nature of God).*

2 Bear (take away, remove, carry off) one another's burdens, and so fulfill the law of Christ."

You would do well to go and read what Paul wrote about love in 1 Corinthians 13. The whole chapter is devoted to walking in love. **And don't do window-shopping when you read it either, *this is who you <u>are</u>*, not who you are *going to become* someday!**

Remember…

YOU ***ARE*** A <u>NEW</u> CREATION ***NOW!***

You are your Daddy's child!

You are a partaker of the Divine Nature!

You are made in His image and likeness!

YOU ARE LOVE!

Paul says in Romans 12:1 & 2,

1 *"I beseech you, therefore, brethren, by (in view of) the mercies of God (in view of what God has done for us in Christ) that you present your bodies **a living sacrifice,** holy, acceptable to God, which is your **reasonable** service."*

It is the only logical conclusion to your salvation, *not unreasonable at all.*

2 *"And do not be **conformed**..."*

That means pressured into a mold, shaped, manipulated into an assumed, fake identity; being something you are not.

*"And do not be conformed to this world (and the way they think and act), but be ye **transformed** (by truth) by the renewing of your mind."*

This word *"transformed"* is referring to the process of metamorphosis by which a caterpillar is changed into a beautiful butterfly. Note that the caterpillar was always meant to become a beautiful butterfly. In fact, that caterpillar always was a beautiful butterfly in disguise. *Its true nature came forth in the metamorphosis.*

James 1:18 - **We too believed the Truth *and were brought forth*.**

John declares our absolute victory when he said in John 8:36,

*"Whom the Son sets free **is free indeed.**"*

It is not so much *knowing* the truth in your head, *in your mind,* that sets you free, *but it is* <u>believing the truth</u>, *fully embracing the truth,* <u>in your heart</u> that sets you free!

Paul says in Romans 12:2,

2 "And do not be conformed to this world, but ***be ye transformed by the renewing of your mind**, that you may prove (taste and experience for yourself) what is that good, acceptable and perfect will of God."*

*"...**be ye transformed by the renewing of your mind,** so that you may **prove** (not just taste and experience for yourself, but also to show forth through your life to the world) what the will of God is."*

So that, through encountering your life of love, God's will may become good, acceptable and perfect to them also.

In closing, I urge you to get yourself a copy of *"The Mirror Bible"* available on line at <u>www.Amazon.com</u> and several other book sellers.

If you want me or someone who is part of our team to come to where you are, anywhere in the world, and give a talk or teach you and some of your friends about the gospel message and this magnificent work of redemption, simply contact us at www.LivingWordIntl.com …or you can always find me on Facebook.

If you have been helped, or your perspective on life has changed as a result of reading this book, please get in touch with me and let me know.

I would love to share your joy *…so that my joy in writing this book may be full!*

"For this reason I bow my knees
to the Father of our Lord Jesus
Christ,
from whom the whole family
in Heaven and earth **is named,**

that He would grant you,
according to the riches of His
glory,
to be strengthened with might
through His Spirit
in your inner man, (His Spirit
uses His Word to do this)
that Christ may dwell in your
hearts through faith;

that you may be rooted
and grounded
in Love,

and may be able to comprehend
together with all the saints

the width, length, depth, and
height of it – to intimately know
the love of Christ
which far surpasses mere
knowledge;
so that you may be filled
with all the fullness of God."
                        –Ephesians 3:14–19

About The Author

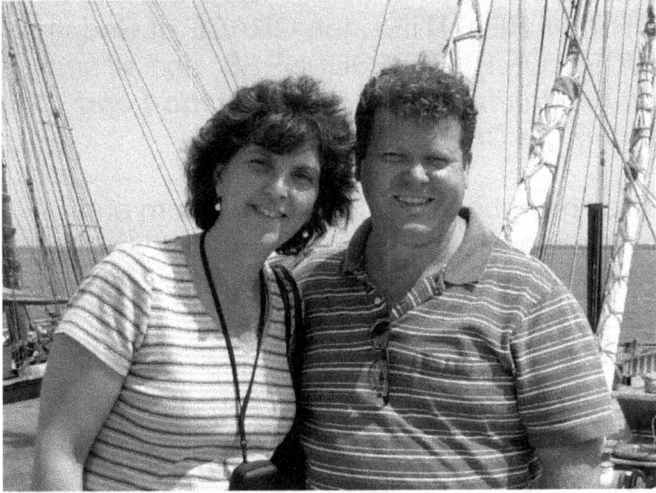

Rudi & Carmen Louw together oversee: Living Word International.

They also travel and minister both locally and internationally.

Rudi was born and raised in the country of South Africa while Carmen grew up in Cortland, New York.

They function in the ministry of reconciliation (2 Corinthians 5:18-21) and flow strongly with the Holy Spirit and His anointing to teach, preach, prophecy, heal, and do whatever is needed, *to touch people's lives with the reality of God's love and power.*

God has given them keen insight into what He has to say to mankind in the work of redemption, *concerning the revelation of, and restoration of,* **humanity's true identity,** therefore they emphasize THE GOSPEL, IN CHRIST REALITIES, the GRACE of God, the WORD OF RIGHTEOUSNESS, *and all such eternal truths* **essential to salvation and living the CHRIST-LIFE**

They have been granted this wisdom and revelation into the knowledge of God by the Spirit of Truth; by the resurrected Spirit of Jesus Christ, *to establish and strengthen believers* **in THE FAITH OF GOD, and to activate them in ministering to others.**

Not only are people set free from the poison and bondage of sin, condemnation and all kinds of intimidation, (upheld, strengthened and reinforced by age old religious ideas, born out of ignorance and deception,) *but many are brought into a closer more intimate relationship with Father God,* **as Daddy,** *through accurate teaching and unveiling of the gospel message, prophetic words, healings and miracles.*

Rudi & Carmen are closely knitted together with several other effective Christians, church fellowships, and groups of believers *who share the same revelation and passion* **to impart the truth of the gospel, so as to impact and transform the world we live in with the LOVE and POWER of GOD.**

www.ingramcontent.com/pod-product-compliance
Lightning Source LLC
Chambersburg PA
CBHW072341100426
42736CB00044B/1668